Martin Monath

Revolutionary Lives

Series Editors: Sarah Irving, King's College, London;
Professor Paul Le Blanc, La Roche College, Pittsburgh

Revolutionary Lives is a series of short, critical biographies of radical figures from throughout history. The books are sympathetic but not sycophantic, and the intention is to present a balanced and, where necessary, critical evaluation of the individual's place in their political field, putting their actions and achievements in context and exploring issues raised by their lives, such as the use or rejection of violence, nationalism, or gender in political activism. While individuals are the subject of the books, their personal lives are dealt with lightly except insofar as they mesh with political concerns. The focus is on the contribution these revolutionaries made to history, an examination of how far they achieved their aims in improving the lives of the oppressed and exploited, and how they can continue to be an inspiration for many today.

Also available:

Salvador Allende:
Revolutionary Democrat
Victor Figueroa Clark

James Baldwin:
Living in Fire
Bill V. Mullen

Hugo Chávez:
Socialist for the
Twenty-first Century
Mike Gonzalez

W.E.B. Du Bois:
Revolutionary Across
the Color Line
Bill V. Mullen

Frantz Fanon:
Philosopher of the
Barricades
Peter Hudis

Mohandas Gandhi:
Experiments in Civil
Disobedience
Talat Ahmed

William Godwin:
A Political Life
Richard Gough Thomas

Leila Khaled:
Icon of Palestinian
Liberation
Sarah Irving

Jean Paul Marat:
Tribune of the French
Revolution
Clifford D. Conner

John Maclean:
Hero of Red Clydeside
Henry Bell

Sylvia Pankhurst:
Suffragette, Socialist and
Scourge of Empire
Katherine Connelly

Paul Robeson:
A Revolutionary Life
Gerald Horne

Percy Bysshe Shelley:
Poet and Revolutionary
Jacqueline Mulhallen

Toussaint Louverture:
A Black Jacobin in the Age
of Revolutions
Charles Forsdick and
Christian Høgsbjerg

Ellen Wilkinson:
From Red Suffragist to
Government Minister
Paula Bartley

Gerrard Winstanley:
The Digger's Life and
Legacy
John Gurney

Martin Monath

A Jewish Resistance Fighter
Among Nazi Soldiers

Nathaniel Flakin

First published in 2018 by Schmetterling Verlag GmbH, Stuttgart as *Arbeiter und Soldat: Martin Monath – Ein Berliner Jude unter Wehrmachtssoldaten*

English-language edition first published 2019 by Pluto Press
345 Archway Road, London N6 5AA

www.plutobooks.com

British Library Cataloguing in Publication Data
A catalogue record for this book is available from the British Library

ISBN	978 0 7453 3996 2	Hardback
ISBN	978 0 7453 3995 5	Paperback
ISBN	978 1 7868 0511 9	PDF eBook
ISBN	978 1 7868 0513 3	Kindle eBook
ISBN	978 1 7868 0512 6	EPUB eBook

Typeset by Stanford DTP Services, Northampton, England

Simultaneously printed in the United Kingdom and United States of America

Contents

List of Abbreviations

AK – *Auslandskomitee* (Foreign Committee) of the IKD, Germany
BDO – *Bund Deutscher Offiziere* (League of German Officers)
Comintern – *Communist International*
Gestapo – *Geheime Staatspolizei* (Secret State Police), Germany
GIM – *Gruppe Internationale Marxisten* (International Marxist
    Group), Germany
IKD – *Internationale Kommunisten Deutschlands* (International
    Communists of Germany)
KPD – *Kommunistische Partei Deutschlands* (Communist Party of
    Germany)
KPO – *Kommunistische Partei-Opposition* (Communist Party,
    Opposition), Germany
LCR – *Ligue Communiste Révolutionnaire* (Revolutionary Communist
    League), France
NKFD – *Nationalkomitee Freies Deutschland* (National Committee for
    a Free Germany)
NSDAP – *Nationalsozialistische Deutsche Arbeiterpartei* (National
    Socialist German Workers Party)
PCF – *Parti Communiste Français* (French Communist Party)
PCI – *Parti Communiste Internationaliste* (Internationalist Communist
    Party), France
PCR – *Parti Communiste Révolutionnaire* (Revolutionary Communist
    Party), Belgium
POI – *Parti Ouvrière Internationaliste* (Internationalist Workers Party),
    France
PSR – *Parti Socialiste Révolutionnaire* (Revolutionary Socialist Party),
    Belgium
SAP – *Sozialistische Arbeiterpartei* (Socialist Workers Party), Germany
SPD – *Sozialdemokratische Partei Deutschlands* (Social Democratic
    Party of Germany)
SWP – Socialist Workers Party, US

Preface

I will never write a book again. This whole process was just exhausting. It was no fun.

Fortunately, with Martin Monath I found a subject who kept me enthusiastic for several years. More than that: I fell in love. There is no academic distance here – I'm an avowed "Monte" fanboy. It is a bit embarrassing to admit how often I clapped with joy while typing on my laptop in a café, or how often I started crying while scribbling in my notebook on the subway.

Why did I fall in love with Viktor, the man of many pseudonyms? Of course I was impressed when I first heard of him: A Jewish Berliner built communist cells in the Nazi army? I have shared his Trotskyist convictions since I was young. But I also find Viktor fascinating because he seems like the exact opposite of me. Viktor always put on a brave face to motivate those around him – I, in contrast, feel compelled to share my neurotic fears. I'm doing it again right now!

This book started as an attempt to make an annotated reprint of the newspaper *Arbeiter und Soldat*. A French translation had appeared in 1978, an English one in 2008, and a partial Spanish one in 2016 – but the original text in German had not been available until I published it last year. For this project, I intended to write a very short introduction about the newspaper's editor. Quickly I discovered that all the available biographical texts offered different "real" names for Viktor – and none of these could be found in the Berlin archives.

I had to dig deeper and deeper. By the time I had finally confirmed the name Martin Monath, after months of searching, I had gathered so much material about the person that I had no choice but to write a book. You will see: This story had to be told. The Trotskyist historian Rodolphe Prager collected lots of materials about Viktor, but it seems he never wrote anything specifically about him. Without his research in the 1970s and 1980s, as well as investigations by Jakob Moneta, Rudolf Segall, and others, this work would not have been possible.

A half-year stay in Mexico City gave me the serenity I needed to write, partially freed from the endless hassles of revolutionary praxis. During my stay I read a book by Argentinean Trotskyist Adolfo Gilly on the Mexican Revolution. He wrote that book in Lecumberri Prison. In the preface he remarked: "Without these years in prison, revolutionary activity would have left me without opportunities nor time nor means for this task."* I feel similarly.

I did most of the writing in the hundreds of Starbucks stores in this gargantuan city. The book would never have been finished without this inexpensive workplace including a regular supply of caffeine. To complete the last few lines, I sat down in the garden of a house in Coyoacán where Leon Trotsky spent his final years. I see the "green strip of grass" that Trotsky described in his testament. Thinking of Viktor's example, I have to agree that life can be beautiful. Since I will only write one book, I am glad it is this one.

A book is never the work of a single person. Many relatives, friends and comrades have also fallen in love with Monte. I would like to thank Naomi Baitner for the stories about an uncle she was never able to meet, and Heidi Sow for the commemorative stone in the sidewalk in Kreuzberg; Angela R. for deciphering the Sütterlin script that was completely illegible to me, and Ursula Martin-Newe and Gertrud Jewan for translations from French; Anton Dannat and Peter Behrens for important tips from the archives of Trotskyism; Marcel Bois and Ralf Hoffrogge for lots of technical pointers for historians; Yossi Bartal and Dror Dayan for translations from Hebrew as well as insights about Zionism; Oskar Huber, Kathrin Kirschner, Stefan Schneider, Neal W., Jana Schröder, Sarah R., and Bethany C. for feedback on the manuscript; and many other people who made this book possible.

---

* Adolfo Gilly, *La Revolución Interrumpida* (México: Ediciones El Caballito 1971), 3 (our translation).

Life is not an easy matter ... You cannot live through it without falling into prostration and cynicism unless you have before you a great idea which raises you above personal misery, above weakness, above all kinds of perfidy and baseness.[†]

†   Leon Trotsky, *Trotsky's Diary in Exile: 1935* (London: Faber and Faber, 1958), 68.

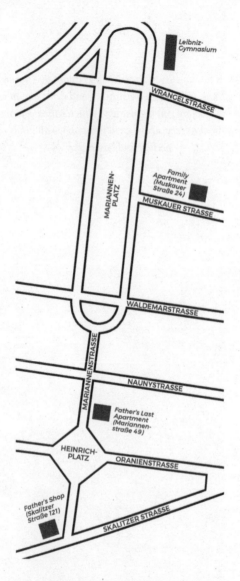

Martin grew up around the Mariannenplatz in the Berlin neighborhood of Kreuzberg.

Map: Nathaniel Flakin.

Dreaming of the European Union of Socialist Council Republics.
Photographer unknown, from the private archive of Naomi Baitner.

PART I
MARTIN MONATH

1

Introduction

1.1. *Almost Like a Tarantino Movie*

It is late 1943 in Brittany in north-western France. For three years the population has been suffering under the Nazis' increasingly brutal occupation regime. In the city of Brest, however, there are astounding scenes of fraternization: Young French workers and equally young German soldiers greet each other with raised fists.[1] An illegal newspaper reports from Kerhuon, ten kilometers from Brest: "On August 6, German soldiers marched through the city and sang the Internationale," the anthem of the revolutionary workers' movement.[2] Between 25 and 50 German soldiers from the Brest garrison had organized themselves into illegal internationalist cells.[3] They obtained identification cards and weapons for the French *résistance*. They felt so confident that they began to ignore the basic rules of conspiracy. They met in groups of ten. "It was madness," recalled their comrade André Calvès, decades later.[4]

At the end of the First World War, millions of German soldiers were infected with socialist ideas. They marched through Germany's streets with rifles and red flags, demanding a republic based on workers' councils. In contrast, the Wehrmacht, the German army of the Second World War, appears monolithic – fanatical down to the last man. This widespread perception makes it fascinating to see dozens of soldiers from the Brest garrison organized in the spirit of socialist revolution. Their enthusiasm – which quickly led to exuberance – cost them their lives. On October 6, 1943, ten (or perhaps 17) of them were shot, together with French activists.[5] The files from the *Reichskriegsgericht* (Reich Court Martial) cannot be found.[6] Yet the judges surely wondered: Where had the young *Landser* (soldiers) gotten such strange ideas?

These soldiers were guided by a strategic vision: The war would lead to a German and European revolution, similar to what happened in 1918–19. This was the perspective in the newspaper *Arbeiter und Soldat* (German: *Worker and Soldier*), whose first issue appeared in July 1943. In Brest, the 23-year-old postman Robert Cruau, a local official of the Internationalist Workers Party (POI), distributed the newspaper to German soldiers. Yet Cruau did not write the articles himself. The newspaper was inspired by Leon Trotsky, the exiled leader of the Russian Revolution and founder of the Fourth International. By this time, however, Trotsky had been buried under the soil of Coyoácan, Mexico, for more than three years. The political leader of this illegal newspaper and conspiratorial network of German soldiers was a 31-year-old Berliner living in a house in the 14th arrondissement (district) of Paris. His comrades knew him as "Viktor."

In his free time, Viktor attended classical music concerts in Paris. His housemate asked if it bothered him – as a Jew – to be surrounded by Nazi officers. "I don't see them at all," Viktor replied, "I only hear Beethoven."[7] Imagining Viktor in a Parisian concert hall, one involuntarily thinks of the climax of the film *Inglourious Basterds* by Quentin Tarantino. But unlike Eli Roth's *Bärenjude* and his fictitious comrades, Viktor didn't want to fight against the Nazis with a bomb. He was aiming for a revolutionary uprising of the working masses.

Viktor's appearance must have seemed like a cliché from an antisemitic fever dream: Slender build, high forehead, hooked nose, wide ears and such shabby clothes that friends later recalled him as a "sort of predecessor of today's hippies."[8] Viktor was poor but well educated: He studied mathematics, composed music, wrote plays, and also worked on a farm for a year to learn about agriculture, while lecturing on Marxist theory. He was rootless, without a native land. He lived where he could serve the revolution. He had taken on the task of subverting the Wehrmacht because his native tongue was German. As an adult, he additionally taught himself Hebrew, Polish, and French. Learning a new language is like a "second birth," he wrote enthusiastically to his brother.[9]

Viktor was a revolutionary. For years he fought for a mixture of Jewish nationalism and utopian socialism as a leader of the Zionist youth movement. But shortly before the outbreak of the war, he became an internationalist communist. Soon he was elected a leading member of the Fourth International in Europe. Viktor stood up for the rights of the Jews – but also for the rights of ordinary German soldiers whom he hoped to win over for the cause of revolution. When he was arrested and tortured by the French police, they asked him if he was Jewish. His answer: "I'm proud of it."[10] At 31, he was executed – twice.

In the 1970s, his childhood friend Paul Ehrlich tried to collect testimonies about Viktor. This work is like a "jigsaw puzzle," he wrote, "because each person only remembers a small piece."[11] Today, several decades later, the problem is significantly more complicated. Using as much information as is ever likely to be available, this book presents a reconstruction of this short life in the service of revolution.

1.2. In the Jungle of Pseudonyms

The historian Wolfgang Abendroth wrote about Richard Müller, the leading figure of the Revolutionary Stewards during the German November Revolution: "Then all traces of him are lost to history."[12] With Viktor, we have the opposite problem: The circumstances of his death are fairly well documented but the further we try to follow his revolutionary career backwards, the blurrier the traces become. Even his real name was hard to ascertain – a result of so much of his life spent underground. More than 30 years after his death, Viktor's comrade Ernest Mandel praised his courage: "He was far from impressed by the Germans. [...] He already had long experience of clandestine activities."[13]

Many names have been passed down for Viktor. The Thalmanns, who shared a house with him in Paris in 1943–4, ended their recollections of him with the sentence: "Viktor's real name was: Paul Wittlin."[14] But that was neither his first nor his last name. In the biography of Ernest Mandel, as in other sources, we find a different spelling: "Paul Widelin."[15] In two obituaries published in the US Trotskyist newspaper *The Militant* in 1946, he was called "Martin

Widelin."[16] One of these articles was a translation from the French Trotskyist paper *La Verité*, except there he was called "Marcel Widelin."[17] Rudolf Segall, who was active with Viktor in the early 1930s, named him in a 2006 interview: "Martin Monat."[18] This name has been used more consistently in recent years.[19]

Since 2016 there has been a commemorative stone (*Stolperstein*) in front of the Muskauer Straße 24 in the Berlin neighborhood of Kreuzberg. The inscription reads: "Martin Monath, born 1912."[20] However, no official records can be found under that name.[21] Only under yet another name was he known to the Berlin authorities – we will return to this question later. For now we can say: Viktor was born as Martin Ludwig Monath in 1913.[22] In this work, we will use the name that Viktor himself used at each stage of his life: first Martin, then Monte, then Viktor.

2

A Jewish Boy from Berlin

2.1. "Robbed of the joys of childhood": Youth

Martin Ludwig Monath, born on January 5, 1913 in Berlin, was a child of war and revolution. At one and a half, he would not have remembered the outbreak of the First World War and the collapse of the Socialist International. Still, he must have had vague memories of the growing hunger of the war years. Martin was five and a half when a wave of insurrections toppled Kaiser Wilhelm II. On that day even the right-wing Social Democrat Philipp Scheidemann was forced to proclaim: "The old and the rotten has collapsed! [...] Long live the new!" The young Martin must have absorbed a central tenet of Marxism: Every political regime is historical, even transient. Or as Bertolt Brecht put it later: "What is certain is not certain. Things will not stay as they are."[1]

We have hardly any sources about Martin's youth, but we know a lot about his generation. The communist Paul Frölich described this generation in a eulogy for his comrade Heinz Behrendt, who was born a year after Martin:

> This generation [...] was robbed of the joys of childhood. They grew up starving, surrounded by grief and fear. [...] This generation went through school and youth as Germany was shaken by severe social and political crises, as inflation and the great economic crisis robbed and uprooted entire classes, millions and millions were unemployed for years and all of society fell into marasmus [undernourishment]. [...] When they finished school, they joined the army of the unemployed by the hundreds of thousands. [...] This was the curse that struck these young people: They were

condemned to idleness and the desolation of their souls. The hope-lessness of this life mocked them year in and year out.[2]

According to Frölich, only a few from this generation could rise above this cruel fate – namely the revolutionaries, "who found the strength to rebel against this lot, to give their lives a meaning by dedicating them to the struggle for a meaningful world."[3]

Despite the lack of sources, we can reconstruct the following about Martin's childhood: In 1904, Baruch Monath moved from Ternopil (then in Austria-Hungary, now in Ukraine) to Berlin, together with his wife Emilie (née Türkischer).[4] Baruch had been born in 1876 to parents who had married in a synagogue, which would later cause problems for their descendants.[5] Baruch and Emilie opened a shop in a middle-class Jewish neighborhood in Berlin, and before long had children. Their daughter Charlotte (Lotte) was born on August 2, 1904.[6] Two sons followed: Martin Ludwig on January 5, 1913, and Karl Artur on August 12, 1915 (see Figure 1).[7] The Monath family was stateless, at least after a certain point.[8] They probably lost a country of citizenship with the collapse of the Austro-Hungarian Dual Monarchy. In a court document, the father was described as a "foreigner (Galician)."[9] The Registry Office of Treptow-Köpenick confirmed that it is in possession of Monath's birth certificate but refused to release it over several months of correspondence.[10]

How does a personality form that is willing to voluntarily fight the murder apparatus of the Nazis, and even to laugh in the faces of its henchmen? Martin's childhood was marked by suffering and death. In 1918, his mother Emilie died – in the years after the First World War, up to 50 million people fell victim to the Spanish flu, twice as many as in the war itself. Baruch Monath remarried but Martin's first step-mother, Sarah, died in childbirth just one year later.[11] Martin's second stepmother – Betty Monath, née Braun[12] – was "very bad" and beat her two stepsons "black and blue."[13] Martin hated this "domineering person [...] with all his heart."[14] On June 28, 1924, when Martin was eleven, his stepmother gave birth to his half-brother Walter.[15]

Shortly before her death, his mother Emilie wrote a letter to her 12-year-old daughter Lotte. "Take good care of your brothers, because your father is very weak." Lotte took this wish to heart.[16] Little Martin

Figure 1   Martin with his little brother Karl
– a child of war and revolution.

Photographer unknown, from the private archive
of Naomi Baitner.

became defiant, with a burning conviction that one has to rebel
against unjust authorities.

Bernhard Monath (a German version of the father's name) ran a
shop for men's attire in the Kreuzberg neighborhood, "a small clothing
store for proletarian customers," as Ehrlich recalled: "His father lived
in constant fear of burglars, and [Martin] often had to sleep in the
shop, sometimes with me keeping him company. We talked all night
and engaged all kinds of tomfoolery."[17]

This shop, at Skalitzer Straße 122 in Kreuzberg, was mentioned in
the Berlin Address Directory for the first time in 1904. It remained
there, or one door down, until 1930.[18] Originally the family must

have lived in the back of the shop. A separate home address is listed for the first time in 1915, first at Parkstraße 2 in Treptow[19] and from 1917 at Muskauer Straße 24 in Kreuzberg. Ehrlich spoke of "conditions of poverty," but the family also had a certain stability. The store remained in the same spot for at least 24 years – through wars, crises, and revolutions. But even in good times, the life of the petty bourgeois is plagued by constant uncertainty. Martin must have felt a deep aversion to the world of Jewish merchants. His alienation from his father's lifestyle might have been a source of the passion that later drove Martin as a revolutionary – first in the struggle for a new life for the Jews, then in the struggle for a new life for all people.

The stability did not last. Even before the global economic crisis, Bernhard Monath went bankrupt. On February 14, 1928, there was a court auction of the "Bernhard Monath Company at Skalitzer Str. 123." According to the court records, the merchant had "already been reported to the public prosecutor's office for fraud by two parties," and "roughly 20 German companies have been defrauded by Monath for about 35,000 marks." On May 13, 1930, the GmbH (limited liability company) was dissolved.[20] What this bankruptcy meant for Martin is unclear. From 1929, the directory listing for Bernhard Monath's business mentions a "successor Elias Schor," and after 1930 the business disappeared for good. An entry for Bernhard Monath at Muskauer Straße 24 can still be found in 1932, and then he appears one last time in 1935 at Mariannenstraße 49. He died in 1936, at 59, of unknown causes, and was buried in the Jewish Cemetery in Berlin. His widow Betty lived with their son Walter at Skalitzer Straße 41, where a last entry appears in 1938. According to the Memorial Book of the Federal Archive of Germany, Betty Wittlin, née Braun, emigrated to Great Britain on February 22, 1939, perhaps at the same time as her son, but was also deported to Auschwitz on March 4, 1943.[21] Why she returned to Germany remains a mystery.

Despite his difficult childhood, Martin was a brilliant student. Paul Ehrlich, who was related to Martin via their grandparents and went to school with him "from the Sexta to the Abitur" (roughly from sixth to thirteenth grade), described him thus:

I can express my memories of [his] personality only with super-latives. He was of an unusual intelligence, always original, and he had the ability to grasp the fundamentals of problems. He was an insatiable reader, and his bag, always packed with books, was notorious in the youth movement. He read everything, but especially philosophy. I remember when he was perhaps 15 or 16, he discovered the French positivists and devoured the works of Auguste Comte (countless volumes). He dragged me to the Berlin City Library again and again to show off his new discoveries. He had an astonishing ability for abstraction, thus also an ingenious talent for mathematics. While we were still in school, he explained problems of modern mathematics to me, the meaning of which I only grasped much later. What would have become of him if he had remained alive? A revolutionary leader of the first order? Or maybe one of the great mathematicians?[22]

Martin was not interested in his looks: "[He] didn't care, really not even a little, about appearances. I wasn't too concerned about my looks either, but compared to him I must have looked like a dandy. He was always disheveled, unkempt [...]. A kind of predecessor of the modern hippies"[23] (see Figure 2).

His little brother Karl described him similarly in a report to their sister: "He doesn't look very good" due to his "irregular lifestyle."[24] Now we can wonder what "disheveled" might mean by modern standards. On the few photos that we have, we see an orderly young man in a suit and tie, with a wristwatch and finely groomed hair. However, we can take Ehrlich at his word that these photos were the absolute exception.

Martin attended the *Gymnasium*, Germany's advanced secondary school. The old Leibniz-Gymnasium at the Mariannenplatz was just a few blocks from his apartment and had many students of Jewish faith.[25] His sister Lotte later told her daughter not to copy answers at school. Uncle Martin had once let a classmate copy the solution to a math problem, and the teacher knew immediately: "Only Martin could have found this solution."[26] Before graduating, the two friends Monath and Ehrlich were expelled from school together for "activities against the school authorities."[27] They had to take their *Abitur* (final

Figure 2   Martin's childhood friend later recalled:
"[He] didn't care, really not even a little, about
appearances. [...] He was always disheveled, unkempt
[...]. A kind of predecessor of the modern hippies."
Photographer unknown, from the private archive of Naomi
Baitner.

exams) as outside students. No records of their graduation remain.[28]
Around 1931–2, Martin enrolled at the Technical University (*Hochschule*), attending the math lectures of Professor Rudolf Rothe. He
wanted to get a degree in engineering, but dropped out in 1933 or
1934.[29] This was a time when hundreds of left-wing and non-Aryan
students were driven out of the university.[30] Unfortunately all these
records are lost as well.[31] Martin never did get a degree, even though
he tried to continue his studies in Belgium and France, almost until

his death. The war and exile got in the way, and even before power was handed over to the Nazis, politics was at the center of Martin's life.

2.2. "From Abel to Bebel": Politicization

May 1, 1933 in Berlin. "The Day of National Labour." Hitler had been Reich Chancellor for three months. The Communist Party of Germany (KPD) had been prohibited for six weeks. The occupation of the trade union houses by the SA (the Nazis' paramilitary *Sturmabteilung*) was planned for the following day. In the morning, hundreds of thousands of people gave the Hitler Salute at a youth rally in the *Lustgarten*, where the 85-year-old Reich President Paul von Hindenburg called for "manly discipline and a spirit of sacrifice." Later, more than a million people gathered at the *Tempelhofer Feld*, with spotlights illuminating the giant swastika banners behind the tribune. In the evening, Hitler proclaimed the end of the class struggle and the beginning of Germany's *Volksgemeinschaft* (national community).[32]

On this day, a guard stood watch in front of the house of the Zionist youth movement Hashomer Hatzair (Hebrew: The Young Guard) in East Berlin. A string led up to the third floor, where a bell was attached. Above, a functionary of the group spoke about the significance of Karl Marx's ideas. In this house, the class struggle lived on, despite Hitler. After the speech, there was a revue – "From Abel to Bebel" – written by the speaker himself. Had a gang from the Hitler Youth showed up, the guard would have rung the bell and the participants would have quickly changed the subject.

The speaker's name was "Monte." The brothers Martin and Karl Monath had both become functionaries of Hashomer Hatzair, and had started referring to themselves as "Monte" and "Carlo." Rudolf Segall attended this meeting on May 1, 1933, as a boy – and he recalled the scene in an interview almost 70 years later.[33]

A Trotskyist obituary for "Martin Widelin" in 1946 said that he entered the workers' movement at age 15. After "five years as an organizer amongst the Berlin youth," when Hitler came to power, "under cover of sports organizations he continued indefatigably to propagate socialism."[34] This is not quite accurate – every reader of the obituary would assume this Widelin was a socialist or communist functionary. But he was in fact a Zionist.

We only know fragments about Monte's initial politicization. Ehrlich reported: "As 12 or 13-year-olds we joined the *Blau-Weiß*, then later to Kadimah, Hazofim, Hashomer Hatzair."[35] This sentence contains a short history of the Zionist youth movement in the Weimar Republic. The Blau-Weiß (German: Blue-White) was a Jewish youth movement, founded by Zionists in 1912 but committed to "general Jewish education."[36] Kadimah (Hebrew: Forwards) was a Zionist youth movement that in 1926 decided to devote itself to problems in the diaspora rather than the colonization of Palestine. As a result, some 150–200 Berlin members of Kadimah left and founded Hazofim (Hebrew: Scouts) with a socialist Zionist profile. In 1931, Hazofim dissolved itself and merged with another faction of Kadimah in Berlin to form the German section of Hashomer Hatzair.[37]

"The Young Guard" was an international organization founded in Poland in 1913. By 1919, their first settlers traveled to Palestine to establish *kibbutzim* (Hebrew: gatherings, i.e. collective farms).[38] By the late 1920s, the group developed its own particular Marxist-Zionist ideology – its goal was a socialist Palestine on a binational, Arab-Jewish basis[39] – and had up to 70,000 members worldwide, including 250 in Berlin.[40] From Ehrlich's remark we can deduce that he and Monte were active in Berlin's Zionist youth movement through a series of splits and fusions, always sticking with the faction that most consistently promoted emigration to Palestine. These groups organized scouting activities, sporting and cultural events, as well as education seminars (see Figures 3 and 4). In Hashomer Hatzair, religion was frowned upon – it was in this group that Ehrlich, seduced by Monte, ate *treyf* (non-kosher food) for the first time. And it was where both of them "made the acquaintance of Marxism" for the first time. Monte served as a *madrich* (Hebrew: youth leader) in the group's Berlin *ken* (Hebrew: nest, i.e. branch).[41] He also lived in a *beth chaluz* (house of pioneers) in Berlin.[42]

What was Hashomer Hatzair's strategic project? In this period there were two movements that promised European Jews an end to their oppression: Zionism and socialism. The "socialist Zionism" of Hashomer Hatzair attempted to reconcile these opposing tendencies.

Figure 3 (left)   The Berlin branch of Hashomer Hatzair on an excursion –
Monte in the center.

Photographer unknown, from the private archive of Naomi Baitner.

Figure 4 (right)   Another excursion of Hashomer Hatzair – Monte on the
bottom left, his brother Carlo at the top in the center.

Photographer unknown, from the private archive of Naomi Baitner.

On the one side was Zionism, founded by Theodor Herzl, a bourgeois response to antisemitism in Europe. It was an attempt to create a new capitalist nation-state in which Jews could live among themselves. Until the Second World War, Zionism represented only a small minority of European Jews. On the other side were socialist movements that propagated a universalist response to antisemitism. Socialist Jews sang songs against the "Narishe Tsienistn" (Yiddish: foolish Zionists): Instead of emigrating, they wanted to fight alongside other workers in their countries for liberation.[43] Zionism regarded the bourgeoisie as the decisive social subject – socialism was oriented toward the proletariat. The socialist Zionism of Hashomer Hatzair and similar groups fell between these two stools and based itself on people from intermediate social layers – people like Monte. They were too battered by the economic crisis to place their hopes in a new capitalist nation-state – but they were too distant from the workers' movement to join a socialist or communist party. (These parties were by no means free of antisemitism either.)[44] Thus a strange mixture emerged: The goal was a new, majority Jewish society, but on a non-capitalist, collectivist basis. And this hybrid included its own hybrids, because many young Jews were simultaneously active in socialist and left Zionist organizations. Socialist Zionism as a mixed ideology was soon pulverized between its two contradictory poles – bourgeois nationalism and proletarian socialism – as we shall see below.

It is no coincidence that this ideology won many followers among Polish Jews in particular, as Ernest Mandel analyzed:

The Jews of Poland, victims of every political and social crisis, who had witnessed pogroms under the Czars, under the revolution, under the Whites, under the Russians, under the Poles, under the Ukrainians and under the Lithuanians, sought a desperate solution through the formulation of a nationalist myth of their own: Zionism. An expression of the complete blind-alley in which Jewish petty bourgeois thought had arrived, this reactionary Utopia was, nevertheless, among the youth and above all the proletarian youth, an expression also of the will to realize the socialist ideal, to participate actively in the world proletarian struggle.[45]

It may sound incredible that in mid-1933 in Berlin, a socialist Jewish youth organization could work openly, and even give a semi-public lecture about Marx. But the Zionist groups in Germany – unlike the Social Democratic Party of Germany (SPD), the KPD, the trade unions, and other workers' organizations – were legal far beyond 1933. Segall commented: "The Zionist groups enjoyed a very 'benevolent support' by the National Socialists [until 1937] because they were the ones who brought Jews out of Germany. The Nazis initially regarded this as quite positive. Here was an organized movement that encouraged emigration to Palestine."[46]

It would go far beyond the scope of this book to investigate the complex relationship between Zionism and National Socialism. Here we will only briefly refer to a statement by Alfred Rosenberg in a book printed by the central publishing house of the National Socialist German Workers Party (NSDAP) in 1937: "Zionism must be actively supported in order to transport a certain number of German Jews each year to Palestine, or generally across the border."[47] For the Nazi ideologue, Zionism was an alternative to Jews spreading "the call for internationalism in the sense of anti-nationalism" and "for class struggle in the sense of civil war."[48] In Rosenberg's eyes, the October Revolution in Russia was part of a Jewish world conspiracy, which he wanted to fight by supporting Zionism. Winston Churchill had formulated a similar idea in 1920.[49]

But Zionism itself was not free of Marxist influences. Monte was not an outlier in this respect, but a member of the national leadership of Hashomer Hatzair in Germany. A former member of the group recalled the conspiratorial Marxist education program which eventually drew the attention of the German authorities: "The Gestapo would come to our programs to see if we were teaching things that were not allowed. Bible and Jewish studies were allowed actually, but Karl Marx was totally banned."[50] It was not until 1937–8 that the Zionist organizations in Germany – both right wing and left wing – were liquidated.

This long tolerance for Zionism meant that articles by Leon Trotsky were still being legally distributed in Nazi Germany at the end of 1933 – but only in Hebrew. The central organ of Hashomer

Hatzair was printed in Warsaw and shipped to Germany. In issues number 13 from October 1933 and number 14 from November 1933, a two-part article by Trotsky appeared under the headlines "Chances in Germany" and "When will the end come?"[51] In this article, Trotsky polemicized against the Communist International (Comintern) and the KPD, who believed the Hitler regime would quickly collapse because of its internal contradictions. The Stalinists expected mass anti-fascist struggles in the near future, and proclaimed that "the struggle for the dictatorship of the proletariat stands in Germany on the order of the day."[52] Trotsky, in contrast, analyzed that "doubtless the most significant defeat in the history of the working class" in Germany had taken place, from which it would not recover quickly. Against the Stalinists' fantastical optimism, Trotsky called for a "revolutionary realism" that recognized the "embittered passivity" in the German workers' movement: "The worker resents the fact that besides Hitler's knout [whip] he is also being driven by the knout of false optimism. He wants the truth. The crying contradiction between the official perspective and the real state of affairs can result only in further demoralization in the ranks of the advanced workers."[53]

Only an earnest balance sheet of the defeat – including of the Stalinists' devastating "theory of social fascism" which had made a united front against the Nazis impossible – could prepare the working class for future struggles against the Hitler regime. For several years, Trotsky had fought for the reform of the Comintern. He wanted the communist parties to return to their foundational principles. But after this defeat without a struggle, and especially after the refusal of the Comintern to draw any kind of lessons, Trotsky recognized the need for the construction of a new revolutionary party. Segall recalled:

> In 1933/34 in Berlin, we were in the unusual position of being able to read the political assessments of Leon Trotsky without belonging to the illegal organization. The magazine of "Hashomer Hatzair" was printed in Warsaw in Hebrew and sent to Germany. Among the articles printed there were works by Trotsky from 1933 and 1934 about Hitler Germany – and Monte sat down with us and translated them for us. These articles made a big impression on us.[54]

Monte had taught himself Hebrew and thus gained access to revolutionary ideas that could otherwise only be found in the underground. Yet Segall's memory seems to have exaggerated the truth: This newspaper contains only a single article from Trotsky's pen. Besides the article we have just quoted, there is only one further reference to Trotsky.[55] It is nonetheless astounding that such texts were available legally in the Third Reich.

The newspaper of the German Trotskyists, *Permanente Revolution*, was prohibited at the end of February 1933. A replacement publication, *Unser Wort (Our Word)*, was printed in Liberec (Reichenberg) in Czechoslovakia beginning in early March and smuggled into Germany, with 1,500 to 2,000 copies per issue.[56] There is no indication that Monte and his friends were familiar with this publication.

Segall met Monte in 1933 and considered him an "astounding Marxist." He assumed: "He and his friend Paul Ehrlich must have had good connections with the communists beforehand."[57] But that's unlikely. Ehrlich reported that Monte began to sympathize with the KPD starting in 1932, while Ehrlich came into contact with the Trotskyist opposition at the university (where he also studied mathematics). How close were these contacts? Did they extend into the time of illegality? We do not know. Ehrlich only wrote that he had read some of Trotsky's pamphlets ("about Germany, social fascism etc."). These pamphlets were distributed in large numbers, far beyond the membership of the Trotskyist organization and its periphery, even into circles of the SPD und the KPD.[58] Ehrlich tried to convince his friend of Trotskyist positions: "Monte listened to me attentively, but did not respond. It was therefore a great satisfaction for me when much later I heard about Monte's development. I saw that as a kind of telepathy."[59]

Monte's membership in Hashomer Hatzair does not preclude membership in a socialist organization. In his youth, the German Trotskyist Jakob Moneta was active in Hashomer Hatzair and simultaneously in the Socialist Youth Organization (SJY), the youth wing of the Socialist Workers Party (SAP). According to Moneta, such dual memberships were the case "for a whole range of people."[60] But despite many points of contact, Monte's interest in Trotskyism – not only as an idea, but as an organization – can only be established starting in 1939–40. Monte was familiar with Trotsky's proposals in 1933: patient underground work in Germany to build a new revolutionary party and a Fourth International. But Monte was not interested. His eyes were fixed on Palestine.

2.3. *"Our hands have become rougher": Denmark*

"Milking, reaping, ploughing, operating machines" – this is how Monte, son of a merchant and student of mathematics, described his daily life in 1934.

Hachshara (Hebrew: preparation) was the term for the agricultural training program to prepare young Zionists for the colonization of Palestine. Jewish youth, mostly from the cities, moved to the countryside in groups to make themselves not only good farmers, but also good Jews. They studied the Hebrew language as well as agronomy. In 1934, about 3,500 German Jews were in the *hachshara* centers in Germany and neighboring countries.[61] Monte's group moved to a farm in Faxe in Denmark (on Zealand south of Copenhagen) and stayed there for over a year (see Figure 5). We even know the exact address from a letter Karl Monath sent to his sister Lotte: The young Zionists lived with Siegwald Haksbjerg in Hyllede, six kilometers from the village of Faxe.[62] Here, Monte wrote a four-page "Letter from the Hachshara" for the organization's yearbook – the first written source we have from him.[63]

In this letter, we can observe Monte's "astounding ability for abstraction" for the first time. He explicitly refrains from writing a "kibbutz chronicle" and reciting the most important events. Instead, the text consists of a philosophical reflection about the relationship of the individual to the collective in the kibbutz. Monte first describes the difficulties of the "easiest, yet most mind-numbing activities, such as hoeing beets [...], where one has to repeat the exact same movement day in and day out." For the young intellectuals this was even more difficult than hard physical labor. But Monte was determined to escape a "typical Jewish" fate:

> Our hands have become rougher and harder: workers' hands. They remind us that we have made good progress on the path from intel-

Figure 5 A goodbye *mesiba* (Hebrew: party) for Monte, who is playing the guitar.

Photographer unknown, from the private archive of Naomi Baitner.

lectuals to workers. But the best proof is not the roughness of our hands, but our productivity. And here I have pleasant news for you. A large part of our group is as productive in all jobs [...] as the Danish farmhands.

Let's pause to take note of the contrast between the young left Zionist Monte and the older (but still quite young) Trotskyist Viktor. Viktor wanted, like countless Jewish revolutionaries before him, to use his position as an intellectual to organize workers. Monte, in contrast, wanted to make himself a worker – and not even a modern industrial worker, but rather a farmhand!

Here we see the utopian strategy of socialist Zionism in a nutshell: Left Zionists from Hashomer Hatzair and similar organizations shared the Zionist objective of a Jewish colonization of Palestine. But instead of a capitalist colony under the patronage of an imperialist power, they wanted to construct a socialist society in the Holy Land. According to this theory, an independent Jewish proletariat would have to constitute itself in the framework of a Jewish nation-state in order to become the subject of a Jewish socialist revolution. The left Zionists found little resonance among the millions of Jewish proletarians in Europe, many of whom were organized in socialist parties and trade unions. Instead, idealistic young Zionists were supposed to transform themselves into new workers. For some, this illusion shattered almost as soon as they arrived in Palestine, where they wanted to build socialist collective farms that were based on the exclusion of the indigenous population. For this reason, some people from Monte's group later broke with Zionism. But we'll return to this later.

"The ordinary farmers hardly knew what a Jew was, and we were the first creatures of this breed they laid eyes on. So they formed their picture of a 'Jew' based on us. I can assure you that, in terms of work, they don't think differently about us than they think about themselves." Monte was thrilled to be challenging negative stereotypes about Jews – not just in the eyes of the Danish neighbors, but also in the eyes of the Jews themselves. Through hard physical exertion, they would dispel any clichés about Jews being unwilling to work. With the lack of modesty typical of any 21-year-old revolutionary, Monte wrote to his *chaverim* (Hebrew: friends): "Generations before us have also considered the ideal of a completely communal life. What distinguishes us from them is that we – not least under the pressure of history – are realizing this ideal."

The erudite Monte must have been well informed about Jewish and Christian sects from thousands of years ago that attempted to build communities on the basis of total equality. He would have been aware of the "completely communal life" of primitive communism. But as a political leader, he was eager to convince his supporters of the uniqueness of their project.

The collective life in the kibbutz, along with political education, was supposed to form new human beings. Monte explained his conception of the relationship between the individual and the community with an anecdote:

In a *sicha* [Hebrew: gathering], R. told us that he wanted to buy certain sheets of music so he could practice a piece on the piano that a farmer had made available to us. Our treasury said that there was only enough money to buy a book that we wanted to pass around in the *chevra* [Hebrew: community]. We also know that for R., playing music is almost a necessity of life. Since we didn't need the book immediately, we bought the sheet music. If the view were correct that the individual in the kibbutz is nothing but a fraction bar above the denominator kibbutz, we would have said: "One person wants sheet music, and fifteen want a book. It is clear that the will of the fifteen has priority over the will of a single person." We don't see a contradiction between the objective tasks of the kibbutz and the needs of its individual members, because the fulfillment of these tasks, the objective success of the kibbutz, depends fundamentally on its people. These people are not just parts of the whole. Each is a unit in itself, with personal needs that must be met if they are to be able to fulfill the great objective tasks of the kibbutz.[64]

But there is no reason to believe that life in the *hachshara* was idyllic. Segall reported, in contrast to Monte's rather abstract reflections, a bit about everyday life: "That was colossally exhausting. We were spread out among the farms and the farmers exploited us quite well. We got almost nothing for our work. What little wage we got went into the group treasury."[65]

Once or twice a week, there were group evenings with intensive political education. Monte was usually the teacher. His friends saw him as a universal genius: He studied mathematics, composed songs on the guitar, and played chess after working all day on the field. Half the group consisted of women, which made the farmers in the area suspicious. But the young Zionists were not in Denmark to make friends. They wanted to get to Palestine as quickly as possible. The *hachshara* was set to conclude with a theater performance in Copenhagen. Monte wrote a play and the group rehearsed it thoroughly, but it was never performed.[66]

In 1934, members of the group returned from Denmark to Germany individually. We only know the exact route of Segall. There were warnings that the Nazis would arrest people returning from abroad so after just three days in Germany, he went via Switzerland to Italy. He spent six weeks traveling through Italy and ended up in Trieste, where he had to wait for an immigration certificate from the British authorities to go to Palestine. In 1935, Segall and his wife sailed via Cyprus to Haifa. They took up residence in a new kibbutz of Hashomer Hatzair, the Kibbutz *Bamifne* (Hebrew: turning point, today: Kibbutz Dalia) near Karkur. Other members of the Denmark group landed there as well. Monte, however, did not. He stayed in Germany and had little contact with his comrades. Years later he wrote to Segall that he would not apply for a certificate for Palestine because he "did not want to take this certificate away from anyone else."[67] For half his life Monte had dreamed of Palestine: The olive trees, the sun, the sea. Now, he remained under the gray clouds of Berlin.

2.4. "A little coup de main": Poland

Was it because of the *mischpoke* (Yiddish: family)? We cannot say for certain why Monte never got in Palestine. He postponed his *aliyah* (Hebrew: ascent, a Zionist term for Jewish emigration to Palestine). His sister Lotte and her husband Hans Teppich had emigrated in 1933, while Segall and other comrades arrived in 1935. Monte took his time, as did his brother Karl. His friends never found out why he stayed in Germany. Paul Ehrlich looked into this question in 1970, without success. Despite his grandiose historical aspirations, Monte might have had simple personal reasons.

It is certain that Monte was still active in Hashomer Hatzair in Berlin in 1936. There are recollections of political disputes within the group, but their nature is unclear. Ehrlich was told that the group did everything to keep Monte in its ranks, due to his abilities, but the differences were too great. "The only one who stood by Monte in these discussions was his young girlfriend Lola Aftergut, for whom he had postponed his aliyah" (see Figure 6). Aftergut's parents lived in Poland and she had to return to them around 1936. For Monte, this was the occasion to break with his organization definitively. The two young people hitchhiked to Poland and "disappeared from the scene of Hashomer Hatzair."[68]

We only know a single anecdote about Monte from this time. Ehrlich learned of a "little coup de main"[69] which he found "typical for Monte":

Figure 6   Rudolf Segall wrote of this photo:
"In the original one can barely make out a sign:
'Tropical Fruits'. Who is the girl?"

Photographer unknown, from the private archive of
Naomi Baitner.

Monte was stateless, a particularly vulnerable status during the
Nazi times. For his trip to Poland, however, he needed a Polish
passport. He could only get one with great difficulty from the
Polish consulate if he could prove his Polish descent and command
of the Polish language and culture. Now Monte had been born in
Germany and could not speak a word of Polish. But he was able, in
a single month, to learn Polish and pass all the tests.[70]

Monte must have returned to Germany in 1938.[71] There, the Nazis
changed his name. A paper from the Registry Office of Berlin-Treptow
from February 13, 1939 states laconically: "By order of the Berlin
District Court, Department 500, the following correction is made:

The surname of the children's parents is not 'Monath' but rather 'Witlin'."[72] Bernhard Monath's parents had married in a synagogue. This marriage was retroactively annulled by the Polish and German authorities, so all of their descendants had to take the maiden name of Bernhard's mother. Thus Martin and Karl Monath were forced to take their grandmother's name: "Witlin." Here we have, finally, the source of one of the many pseudonyms: "Widelin" and "Wittlin" are both alternative spellings of this surname. "Martin Witlin" is still listed in the Registry Office in Treptow-Köpenick in Berlin.[73] Monte was able to survive for years as a Jew in the underground in occupied Belgium and France – it is entirely possible that this name change and the resulting bureaucratic confusion were helpful.[74]

During this time in Poland and Germany, Monte kept up with developments in Palestine. His friends were building kibbutzim, socialist agricultural collectives, as they had learned together in Denmark. However, the pioneers soon ran up against the fundamental contradiction of Zionism: the natives. The Zionist trade union Histadrut (Hebrew: federation) advanced the principle of "Hebrew labor." Arab workers were excluded wherever possible. This was an insoluble problem for the socialist Zionists: How could the new society be based on social equality yet also on racial segregation?[75]

In 1936, the Palestinians began an uprising against British colonial rule and Zionist immigration. As Segall recalled in an interview, the idea of peacefully constructing a new Jewish socialist society in Palestine quickly vanished among the young settlers:

> From 1936 onwards, we could only go out to work [on the fields] with armed guards, or carrying weapons ourselves. We surrounded the camp with fortified positions [...] and after work each of us had to stand guard for about two or three hours. Then we each held a hand grenade in our hand, with a rifle standing nearby, and waited for possible attacks.[76]

In the Kibbutz *Bamifne*, with its approximately 100 members, there were sharp discussions about if and how the socialist experiment could continue. Six to eight members decided that the Zionist project was hopeless. "We came to the conclusion that [Zionism's] attitude towards the Arabs could only lead to a calamity," Segall recalled. "The expulsion of Arabs to settle Jews in Palestine, and the prohibition of Arabs working there, cannot continue."[77]

This group became increasingly interested in Trotskyism. Around this time Jakob Moneta, who had emigrated from Germany in 1933, organized joint strikes of Arab and Jewish workers. For this, he was reprimanded by his union, and began searching for a political alternative to left Zionism: "Roughly five comrades eagerly followed all the Trotskyist literature from abroad we could get. We discussed the Spanish Revolution and the Moscow Trials. We ended up in opposition to the leadership of Hashomer Hatzair, which at the time was very pro-Stalinist."[78]

This small group included Monte's childhood friend Paul Ehrlich as well as his comrade Rudolf Segall. They still felt enthusiastic about the collectivist life of the kibbutz, but they no longer considered themselves Zionists. This contradiction was not tolerated. The kibbutz told them: "Either in or out!" Paul Ehrlich capitulated and remained in the kibbutz until his relatively early death. Segall claimed that he simply did not like the kibbutz and left without a discussion. Moneta, on the other hand, raised political criticisms and was expelled. Segall, Moneta, and a few others moved to the city of Haifa, some 50 kilometers away. There they got involved in a Trotskyist discussion group, Chugim Marxistim (Hebrew: Marxist Circles). Members of this group "believed that the [upcoming] war would end with a revolution. So we prepared to return as soon as possible and participate in the revolution in Europe."[79]

After the war, Segall and Moneta did indeed return to Germany where they became leading members of the German section of the Fourth International. Another member of the Haifa group, Yigael Gluckstein, moved to England in 1948 where, under the pseudonym Tony Cliff, he led a large Trotskyist organization until his death in 2000.

Contact between Haifa and Berlin was difficult. Nonetheless, Monte must have had at least a rough idea that some of his comrades, with whom he had done the *hachshara* in Denmark, were disappointed by actually existing Zionism and started down a new political path.[80] Segall's development in Haifa ran parallel to Monte's own break with Hashomer Hatzair in Berlin, even though 2,800 kilometers separated the two former collaborators.

2.5. *"Seek another road!": The* Polenaktion

In late October 1938, the Nazi regime deported thousands of German Jews with Polish citizenship. The *Polenaktion* (German: Poland Action) was in response to a law passed by the Polish parliament which would deprive Poles of their citizenship if they had lived abroad for more than five years. As a result, many Jews living in Germany would have become stateless. Shortly before the law came into effect, the German authorities carried out massive nighttime raids: From October 27 to 29, the Gestapo dragged 17,000 Jews out of their homes and sent them to the Polish border in special trains. Thousands of them were not allowed to enter Poland, however, and were interned by the border police in the village of Zbąszyń (or Bentschen in German).[81]

Among the deportees were Sendel and Riva Grynszpan from Hanover. On the night of October 27, 1938, the Gestapo came to their apartment. Their son Henschel had moved to Paris two years earlier because of the deteriorating situation in Germany. He was living with relatives in the French capital – illegalized, destitute, and stateless, without work, and wanted by the police. On November 3, the 17-year-old received a postcard from his family describing the deportation and the miserable conditions in Zbąszyń. Four days later, he wrote a response to his parents, which he put in his pocket, and walked into the German embassy. Grynszpan said he was in possession of important documents for the ambassador. However, Ambassador Johannes von Welczeck had just left for a walk. Instead, the young man was sent to the Legation Secretary Ernst vom Rath (a junior member of the diplomatic staff). Rath asked for the documents, and Grynszpan drew a revolver. "You're a filthy kraut," he cried, "and now on behalf of 12,000 persecuted Jews, I give you the document!" He fired five times at the fascist official. Then he calmly surrendered to the French police. Two days later, on November 9, Rath died from his wounds. That very night, the state-sponsored pogroms against Jews in Germany – *Kristallnacht* or the "Night of Broken Glass" – began.

The SA and civilians attacked thousands of Jewish homes, businesses, and institutions; 267 synagogues were burned and destroyed. In the following days, 30,000 Jewish men were detained in concentration camps.[82]

A lonely young man had shaken up world politics. Was there more to this than a 17-year-old's desire for revenge? Rumors and speculation spread around the world. On November 9, *L'Humanité*, the central organ of the French Communist Party (PCF), claimed "that young Grynszpan was in constant relation with the Trotskyist circles, which swarm with agents of the Gestapo."[83] This accusation was just as false as so many other Stalinist slanders against the Trotskyists, and the American Socialist Workers Party refuted the claim one month later.[84] Leon Trotsky himself, in his Mexican exile, could not speak about the case until February 1939. He expressed his admiration for the young man: "People come cheap who are capable only of fulminating against injustice and bestiality. But those who, like Grynszpan, are able to act as well as conceive, sacrificing their own lives if need be, are the precious leaven of mankind."[85]

Yet Trotsky was a lifelong opponent of individual terrorism of this sort.[86] "Unfortunately," he wrote, a brave young man like Grynszpan had not found his way into the ranks of the Fourth International, which would have given him different and better weapons to fight against the Nazis. That is why Trotsky combined his moral solidarity with a political appeal to "all the other would-be Grynszpans" in the world: "*Seek another road!* Not the lone avenger but only a great revolutionary mass movement can free the oppressed, a movement that will leave no remnant of the entire structure of class exploitation, national oppression, and racial persecution."[87]

What did all of this have to do with Monte? Among the 17,000 people deported during the *Polenaktion* was Karl Monath, i.e. Monte's younger brother Carlo. He was arrested in Berlin one day after the Grynszpans, on October 28. The police took him to the train station Schlesischer Bahnhof (today: Ostbahnhof) and forced him into a train to the Polish border. He was trapped in Zbąszyń alongside thousands of other deportees. After three months, he and Martin's friend Leo Schiffmann made it to Warsaw, and from there to Vienna. They reached Ancona, on the Adriatic Coast of Italy, and took a cargo ship to Palestine in early 1939. They traveled illegally, without permission from the British colonial authorities – this was known as the "Aliyah Bet."[88] The journey went quickly: After a few weeks Karl arrived in a town 50 kilometers from Jerusalem where his sister Lotte had been living for six years. From there, the siblings wrote to Monte in Berlin.

Monte was a "would-be Grynszpan" who now faced the same decision. It is unlikely that he read Trotsky's appeal (at least not at this time). And yet he was an archetype of Trotsky's target audience. Monte had just turned 26, but was already an experienced political cadre. He had turned away from the Zionist project of colonizing Palestine which had dominated his life for several years. The dream of a new Jewish socialist society in Palestine had shattered due to its inner contradictions. Monte now lacked an orientation: The Holy Land was not an option, but he could not stay in his native Berlin either. "With military precision" he prepared to flee Germany,[89] but Jewish refugees were welcome almost nowhere. Foreign governments took their time with asylum applications while the persecution of Jews in Germany intensified.

Any living and breathing person must have longed for bloody revenge against Hitler and his henchmen. However, for Monte it would have been completely unsatisfactory to limit this revenge to a single Nazi official. No, the people who had brought Hitler to power – the big capitalists, the *Junker* (Prussian landed gentry), and the generals – needed to pay. Monte did not yet know the form his revenge would take. With all his extraordinary intelligence, he set out in search of a strategy.

Every young revolutionary passes through a fanatical phase: A direct assault on all the fortifications of class rule, in the firm belief that the existing social order can be brought down in one sustained push. After this phase, many revolutionaries simply give up. Fewer find the strength for a more extended struggle. Monte had ended this first phase but not yet entered the second. His friends must have thought he had suddenly abandoned politics. Monte was not one to share half-finished thoughts, even within a small circle. Even with his childhood friend Paul or his little brother Karl, he kept every doubt to himself. Only when he had completed a plan would he go out and proclaim it to the world with trumpets blazing. So far, no new plan was ready. The tireless Zionist activist Monte had outlived his usefulness. A few years later, the Trotskyist strategist Viktor appeared in his place. In the meantime, lots of political reflection was necessary. Monte knew his life would remain in the service of "the cause" – but he was not yet sure what exactly this "cause" would be.

3

Letters from Berlin and Brussels

On January 25, 1939, Monte sent a response to his brother in Palestine.[1] This is the first of nine letters Monte wrote to his siblings which have survived until today – the most extensive sources we have from him (except for his later Trotskyist agitation and propaganda).

This first letter is written on stationary of the "Zionist Chapter of Dresden" with a secretariat at Gerichtstraße 27. Monte reported that he had already received news of Carlo's arrival in Palestine "via the group,"[2] meaning he was still in contact with Hashomer Hatzair. Despite the traumatic experiences of the previous weeks, the eloquent and theatrical Monte could not help teasing his laconic younger brother. Apparently, Carlo had described his involuntary trip to the Middle East in few words. Monte wrote:

> [Your message] gave me great pleasure, even more that you enjoy the 'June-ish' sun, even more that you ate, and most of all that you are in a good mood. Given your Protestant temper, I did not expect you to be overcome by holy feelings. [...] My main joy is that you are no longer where you were for so long, unnecessarily complicating my already complicated trains of thought.

Monte was also planning a trip: He wanted to move from Berlin to Paris to continue his university studies. This plan was delayed, however, which is why he simultaneously applied for a permit for London, "which I will receive with 95% certainty [...] in 2–3 weeks." For a Jew in Berlin in early 1939, despair was in order. Yet Monte dedicated himself to the question of where to get a degree. In his free time, he was learning French diligently – which was "a lot of fun," yes "dead certainly more fun than Polish." In a different letter he expressed his boundless joy about the new language: "The first use of a new language is like a second birth. It is the start of a completely new epoch in a person's life. It is the conquest of a completely new part of the world."[3] Monte did in fact have a chance to reinvent himself completely. Soon he would even take a new name.

But first he wrote about "little Walter," who had an "urgent reservation to go to England." Walter, his half-brother, was 14. At the time, the *Kindertransport* (German: children's transport) was halted and the boy was stuck in a queue. Martin and Karl Monath suppressed their worries about their young relatives by exchanging photographs. The whole family were hobby photographers and pictures took up no small part of their correspondence. Unfortunately none of these survive.

Monte's letter also dealt with bureaucratic matters. He had to obtain his brother's birth certificate from the Registry Office of Berlin-Treptow, and also needed permits for his own emigration. The slow workings of the bureaucracy could have literally cost him his life. Yet he remained sanguine. In case he could not acquire Karl's documents before his own departure, Monte wrote that "in the worst case [...] la mère" would send them, i.e. the hated stepmother. Monte, as we already have seen, refrained from making detailed reports. He nonetheless requested a thorough description of his brother's "odyssey," and closed with a "congratulation" in Hebrew. An addendum was addressed to his older sister Lotte: "Maybe the news that I want to study in these times shocks you. But don't get upset, little girl. Trust that there are good reasons that cannot be guessed from over 2,000 kilometers away."

What stands out about this letter are all the things that go unmentioned. The catastrophe was already underway. Tens of thousands of Jews were in concentration camps, tens of thousands more in exile, some of them forcibly deported. The German Reich had already seized Austria and the Sudetenland. Any politically savvy person knew that war was imminent in Europe. Monte was in immediate danger. Not only had his brother been deported, he was also sending his stepbrother into exile while his stepmother was preparing her own escape to England. What did Monte have to say about all this?

"The physical sky corresponds perfectly to the political one, alternating between snow and rain."[4] This was his most severe complaint. The letter's tone is light, almost joyful. Monte's lack of worry seems strange, almost pathological. Of course he was afraid, but he allowed no trace of fear into his letters. He wrote about his siblings' gray cat and did not mention that his acquaintances were being forced to adopt new first names, such as Israel and Sarah.[5] With complete confidence Monte worked on his plans to emigrate.

3.2. *"To strive, to seek, not to find, and not to yield": More Letters from Berlin*

The nine handwritten letters from Monte are on cheap paper, heavily faded, partially cut off, and generally hard to decipher.[6] One is in all likelihood not by Monte at all. They alternate between German and French, with scraps of Hebrew and English. There is talk of aunts and uncles who could not be identified. We possess only one side of the correspondence – the responses sent by Karl and Lotte have been lost. Much remains unclear. Nevertheless, we can learn a lot about Monte.

In a second letter written after Karl's arrival in Palestine, from mid-February 1939, Monte wrote that it was "not necessary" for him to move there. He thanked his brother, assuring him, "It will calm you to know that the road remains open."[7] It is remarkable that a former Zionist leader was now considering every possible destination for exile except Palestine, even though his two siblings were already there.

Karl had trained as a lathe operator after he was kicked out of his high school in Berlin by the new Nazi principal.[8] In Palestine, he first moved into a kibbutz, but quickly left again to become an artisan. Soon he found a job as a metalworker alongside his brother-in-law Hans Teppich.[9] Both brothers were learning new languages: Monte wrote some of his letters in French and his brother replied occasionally in English – partly to practice and partly to avoid censorship.

The brothers corresponded via a "third party," and it could take up to two-and-a-half weeks for letters to arrive. An unnamed "gang of thieves" was responsible for the mail.[10] Monte included return postage for his siblings, "especially as it is less of an imposition to me than ever before." It is not clear where his money came from – he only jokingly refers to a "Finance Committee." In the past he had financed his studies by giving private lessons. Perhaps Monte wanted to downplay his financial concerns in his letters. Instead, he expressed concern for his big sister and little brother, since "you don't live in the safest climate either."[11] He did not write a word about his own difficulties. Reading the letters, one can almost forget the political context: Two weeks before this letter was written, Hitler had given a speech in the *Reichstag* (parliament) threatening "the annihilation of the Jewish race in Europe."

Monte was "a bit proud" of his little brother and reminded him of the epigraph of a book by Romain Rolland: "To strive, to seek, not to find, and not to yield."[12] Despite the adverse circumstances, Karl refused to despair. Both brothers displayed unusual resilience. At the beginning of February, Monte had said goodbye to his half-brother Walter. The *Kindertransport* resumed and Walter made it to England.[13] Despite the growing danger in Berlin, Monte had acquired an encyclopedia as a parting gift for the boy. This required "two hours of travel on the tram, jumping out of moving trains and similar little jokes." For Monte, survival in the Nazi capital was an "adventure" – despite the fact that he was still waiting for answers from foreign governments about his asylum applications. He had expected the permit for England "with 95% certainty" by mid-February. Now it was mid-February and everything could still take "two weeks" or maybe "also 2–3 weeks later." Monte nonetheless put on a carefree face – at most he was concerned about a lack of regular correspondence from his siblings. On February 14, he received Karl's birth certificate and forwarded it immediately. "Long live the Treptow Registry Office!"[14]

In May, Monte dealt with political questions for the first time in his letters. Karl had sent a "rather amusing description of the uprisings in Palestine."[15] This did not refer to the Palestinian general strike which had started in 1936, but rather to protests by Jewish colonists against the White Paper of the British government of Neville Chamberlain, approved by the House of Commons on May 23, 1939. The MacDonald White Paper, named after the British colonial secretary, was an attempt by His Majesty's Government to gain the support of the Arabs in the approaching war. The paper promised the creation of an independent Palestinian state within ten years. Since 450,000 Jews were already living in Palestine, the British government considered its promise of 1917 to create a "national home for the Jewish people" (the Balfour Declaration) to be fulfilled. For the next five years, Jewish immigration was to be limited to a total of 75,000 people. The future Palestinian state would not be a Jewish state since London was opposed to the idea that "the Arab population of Palestine should be made the subjects of a Jewish State against their will."[16] The various Zionist groups in Palestine rejected the White Paper outright and protested against it with demonstrations, strikes, and even bombings.

Monte wrote a letter in French in which he seems no less disappointed than the Zionists. The promises made by the British government were not to be believed: "The example of the Jewish state probably shows the entire world sufficiently how much trust can be placed in the English."[17]

Monte considered the anti-British protests pointless. Despite the limitations on immigration, Jews would continue to reach Palestine illegally – just as Karl had done. He saw no possibility of "influencing the English" with such protests, since they were concerned with major questions of world politics. For him, "the powerlessness of Jewish society" was demonstrated by the fact that "the Jewish question has again been transformed into a philanthropic question, and not a national one." He considered the idea of "getting the masses to rise up and throw bombs, as the neighboring people has been doing for several years." The demonstrations so far seemed "a bit ridiculous," since they avoided clashes with the police and principally damaged Jewish businesses.[18] He did not mention bombings by the right-wing Zionist paramilitary organization Irgun. Monte asked his brother what answer he thought the Jews should give to the White Paper. As was typical in this phase, he offered no thoughts of his own. He was still in the middle of his political metamorphosis. We can already see the seeds of his later development: He had no confidence whatsoever in the diplomacy of the capitalist states, especially not of "democratic" British imperialism. His hopes lay in the action of the masses.

3.3. *"A special treat for an old traveler": Flight to Belgium*

"Why Belgium, and how?" It was late summer of 1939. For months, Monte had written about his preparations to leave for France or England. He was still living with the Blumfeld family at Gutenbergstraße 4 in the Charlottenburg neighborhood, where his brother had also lived until his deportation.[19] Suddenly, his siblings received a letter from Belgium.

Via the Zionist organization Hechaluz (Hebrew: pioneer) Monte had received a permit to go to England, and from there continue to Palestine. But he did not want to go to the Holy Land. His goal was still the university in Paris. Had he gone to England, he would have continued on to France right away.

> There could have been difficulties for [my friends from Hechaluz] if I had immediately disappeared from England. I would have taken someone else's place and their possibility to emigrate. At that time the trip to Belgium was easy and safe. What was more natural, after brief consideration, than for me to reject the gracious offer? For my purposes Belgium is just as good as England. There I might have had to stay in the middle of nowhere just to get a permit, while here legalization is possible without difficulty.[20]

At that time it was relatively easy for refugees from Germany to obtain asylum in Belgium. (Henschel Grynszpan had received a residence permit in Belgium before traveling to France illegally.)

In Brussels, Monte filed an asylum application with the *police des étrangers* (French: Foreigners' Police). He had a deportation order from the German Reich for May 5, 1939, but he had arrived in Belgium on May 1.[21] In his letter to his siblings, Monte had a laugh about his many names – "M. Witlin = M. Monath = Monte, M. Withen thus unknown" – and at this time he was still not living underground. The trip to Belgium had not exactly been easy:

> Since I had been deported and only had a short time left, I had to attempt the crossing regardless of my wishes. I took care of all "business" with complete calm and left. It was, as you can see,

dangerous, romantic, and a special treat for an old traveler. Above all, it worked. [...] From Berlin, I first flew to Hamburg (it had to go very fast since I had things to take care of there, but the flight itself was heavenly).

Using an airplane for travel within Germany might sound surprising. In 1937, the Deutsche Luft Hansa A.G. transported over 300,000 passengers. A flight from Berlin's Tempelhof airport to Hamburg cost 25 Reichsmarks and lasted one hour.[22] Until the last moment Monte wanted his acquaintances to believe he was going to England. Even after the fact he wanted his siblings to claim he had gone first to England and from there to Belgium, "to avoid any conflict." For Monte "the main thing is that I make it to Paris soon."

Paris remained a problem. He had found a place to study, but:

> The professor had to provide a guarantee for my honor. And apparently, a person who is a socialist cannot be honorable. Unfortunately the professor had heard that I worked in a soc[ialist] movement, even in a leading role. He was worried about his standing as a state official and refused. From Berlin, I could not say a word about this. Now I will give him a most solemn promise that I will be abstinent for one year. He only needs to give a guarantee for half a year, and I myself cannot guarantee for more than a year.

By his own account, Monte was no longer politically active in 1939 – but could not promise his inactivity would continue for more than six months. Even in a new city, Monte's optimism was unshakable. In a Berlin dialect he wrote: "This thing is going to work out."[23]

At the time of his flight, Monte had 9,000 Reichsmarks. In 1939, the average annual salary in the German Reich was 2,092 Reichsmarks, so he had earnings from four-and-a-half years in his pocket.[24] How did he get this money? We do not know. It was prohibited for Jews in Germany to take currency outside the country. Monte with his conspiratorial drive found ways to smuggle this small fortune into exile. In Berlin, he purchased internationally coveted stamps – this was "more difficult and more exciting than I had anticipated." He had to speak with an employee of the foreign exchange office "about the Jewish question and currency controls with a cool head, without the swine guessing who I am or what I want." As always, Monte described this life-threatening performance as an adventure: "It was kind of fun and you can thank God that your brother has a sufficient degree of cheekiness." He sent the stamps to Paris and Brussels in different ways, including via the French cultural attaché. As soon as he was able to convert them back into hard currency, the financing of his studies would be secured for several years. This would take some time, however, and at the beginning he had few resources.

It is likely that Monte had transported money for other Jews – he referred to "financiers" that planned to "repay according to urgency." For this project, he had "acquired a dash of expertise in that special idiocy called stamp collecting" and was satisfied with his performance as a "currency smuggler." However, he had already lost interest in this profession: "The only compensation in this case was the danger, as well as the small joy of stealing from the German Reich and its Führer, i.e. taking the spoils of the greatest thief before he could get his claws into them."

The following day Monte left his unknown first location in Belgium and went to Brussels, where French was spoken. He understood that he was much better off than "90% of emigrants" because he was well dressed – "quite decent from my hat to my shoes, with one bourgeois outfit and then a casual one" – and had enough money. At least he claimed that in family circles. He promised further reports for his siblings and made fun of his taciturn brother with his "five-line essays." Even on the run, Monte remained Monte. He valued high culture more than his own life:

In Germany I saw a few nice films, [...] and in the [evening] before my departure I saw The Magic Flute (marvelous!). In the big rush I still found time, 2 x 2 hours [two sessions of two hours each], and a fine music student gave me didactically good lectures about pre-classical and classical music, with examples on the gramophone. I cursed God and the world that we did not have time to get to postclassical music.

3.4. "Dance halls and fairgrounds": Boredom in Brussels

Monte was now in relative safety – and he had nothing to do. For his whole life, the young man with the energy of a hummingbird had kept busy with elaborate plans. His escape from Berlin had been successful; his studies in Paris remained uncertain. The 26-year-old was bored. On July 13, he sent a postcard to Jerusalem – he had "elegantly neglected" to write a letter.[25] At the end of July or the beginning of August, he sent one final letter to his siblings.[26] When the war began, the correspondence broke off.

This letter, filling 18 tightly scrawled pages, is longer than all the others put together. For the first time, Monte gave an account of his daily life in exile. He saw that a horrific war was approaching. Yet he still had no idea how to fight against it.

What was Monte's life in Brussels like? He had been an "appallingly lazy guy" for not writing sooner. His excuse was that he "did not know much to write about that would have been of interest to you." At most he could "swear [...] about these evil times that scatter old acquaintances to the four winds." At the same time, he knew that each letter might be his last chance to "use the possibly very short time before the war." That is why he wrote despite the lack of "revolutionary novelties."

Monte was "quite satisfied" with his "French chattering." He had tried to hire a detective to find the address of a Parisian stamp dealer. He was sure that all the detectives were trying to cheat him with "outrageous prices" and make themselves seem "terribly important," since most of their customers based their expectations on detective novels "instead of inquiring what prices are appropriate." Why did he mention this when he was usually so reserved about his difficulties? It seems he wanted to prove that his knowledge of French was already good enough that he could argue with detectives.

Then he wrote about the opposite gender. His last girlfriend in Germany had "unfortunately and thankfully left with her parents for Shanghai more than a month before me." She was involved in Monte's "illegalities" and he was happy to know that she was now "out of the reach of the German police." In order to meet new girls, he went dancing. In Brussels, the rumba ("an awful dance") and waltzes were popular. Monte had no experience whatsoever. He let a barber from his building drag him to a dance hall. Here, Monte was just as inclined toward strategizing as anywhere else. This work is not a hagiography, so we can look at Monte's "strategies" toward women with distaste for the dehumanizing tone:

> I realized that I would have ruined my chances with every woman after the first dance. So I decided to approach the ugly ones first. Whoever wore glasses, had slightly crossed eyes, was poorly built, had a double chin, elephant legs and such things – they were not safe from my requests to dance. And you can believe me: At first it was no fun at all for them. Success came eventually: After two hours all the girls from the category of the ugly ones (who some lovers would have counted in the category of the beauties) were "danced out." Behold, one could approach the dance beauties peacefully and securely.

Two days later, Monte continued writing his letter. In the meantime his enthusiasm for dancing had grown so much that he instructed his brother to visit "the dance hall from time to time instead of the cinema." Karl could get his sister to "fasten his tie appropriately." Monte felt that people from the German youth movement were "too inhibited" and dancing would help them "loosen up their bodies and possibly their spirits." He was so insistent with his advice that he had to assure his brother that he was not getting a "kickback from the 'dance host'."

The day before, Monte had "passed an aptitude test for the next war, and done very well." Why was a refugee in Belgium being drafted? Monte was only testing his military skills at the *foire*. The Brussels fair took place each summer for six weeks on a central boulevard. Monte felt like a king – as if he were the best at every carnival game – and he shared his unrestrained joy with his siblings. First he was at "a stall at which one had to roll a face in the form of a torpedo up a slanted rail. Anyone who made it to the top had the pleasure of seeing a small firework explode, essentially proclaiming one's competence and strength to the world." Monte watched three soldiers attempt this strongman game. Only the third succeeded, and that after many attempts. When it was Monte's turn, the firework went off on his first try, and then twice more. "In any case, my respect for the uniform was gone," he wrote. Things went the same at the shooting gallery: Twice in a row, Monte hit the bullseye four times and won a bottle of wine. A group of soldiers had again performed worse. Monte, with no military experience, was so proud of his skills that he included the target in the envelope. He could make use of his new-found ability to shoot: "Right into the heart of German discord!"[27]

A day after writing such long-winded and offhand descriptions of his daily life, the young revolutionary felt remorse. "What have I written?" he asked himself. This was a letter the likes of which "is not written in Jewish circles." Now he assured his siblings that he had made a completely false impression of himself: He had only been to the dance hall and the fairground a few times. Every day he was busy with "serious things" and he only went dancing once a week. He listened to music for 1–2 hours per day on an old radio that he had repaired – but only so he could recuperate his strength for the serious things. This brought him back to his passion, classical music, writing about Gounod and Cortot and then repeating the story of the lecture he attended on the day of his escape. "An example of the peace of mind with which I dealt with all the difficulties at that time. Almost like minor points."

Had Monte already begun to move in illegal communist circles in Brussels? He only wrote that he "did not exactly spend his evenings alone," without hinting at what he was up to. In a previous letter, he mentioned going on a camping trip with the "'free' thinking youth" in Belgium on the Pentecost weekend (May 28–9, 1939). Historically this had been a code word for the socialist youth movement. For this, "the Zionist god punished" Monte: he fell into a hole and broke a small bone in his foot.[28]

With his siblings, he emphasized that he was "not a rolling stone." Instead of eating at a restaurant, he prepared his meals at home for little money. In his descriptions of meat, vegetables, and flour he sounds as if he were making exciting scientific discoveries.

In his first three weeks in Belgium he had spent 700 francs, or 100 marks. He had received 50–170 francs "from the comité" – presumably from the *Comité d'Aide et d'Assistance aux Victimes de l'Antisemitisme en Allemagne.*[29] He lived in his own room in an old two-story house, and was gleeful when describing his marble tabletop – "the most beautiful thing" – and his private entrance. In Belgium, unmarried couples were allowed to live together, which Monte found very modern. His window had a view into the garden, and the neighborhood contained mainly old villas. We know his address from a postcard, as well as from his asylum application: Rue de Berger 32, in the city center, not far from the Royal Palace.[30]

Then he remembered to congratulate his siblings for their birthdays. Lotte had turned 35 on August 2 and Karl turned 24 on August 12.

When he finally began to talk about the future, Monte had to confess that things were not going entirely smoothly. "My studies will work out for sure," he affirmed, as always, but he still couldn't find a way to get to Paris. Certain steps of his currency smuggling operation were causing problems. He still had not found the address of the Paris stamp dealer, despite his conversations with detectives, and some of his helpers in Germany had "proven themselves to be not entirely skillful." He had bought a dentistry tool in Germany for 1,000 marks and wanted to convert it back into cash, but it was being held up by customs. His books and clothes from Berlin had not arrived in Brussels either – "two suitcases are enjoying themselves in England." The only suit he owned – "with which I crawled across the border at night" – was in such bad shape that he could not visit consulates or take care of other formalities. Monte did not let such small things spoil his optimism, though. Always the cheerful Jewish atheist, he exhorted his siblings: "Pray for my things at the Wailing Wall!" Monte could not plan his future freely. Any plans:

> must necessarily include the question of a war. It is conceivable that a war could botch up my plans for university studies. There could be a sudden internment of foreigners, or there could be compulsion (more than just moral) exerted on all refugees to join the army (which would still be more pleasant than being forced into the German one). In short, all kinds of things can happen.

But Monte refused to "let himself be distressed" and intended to try "by all means" to continue his studies. Only after finishing a degree would he be ready for the army – "even though I no longer see the point in fighting in a bourgeois army; rather preparing the struggle against it and within it." Monte must have come into contact with revolutionary socialists shortly after his arrival in Brussels. His views were evolving rapidly.

3.5. *"We live in historic times": Trotskyization*

Monte continued his letter, already nine pages in German, with a "political part" in French.[31] Here we see his analysis of world politics in the late summer of 1939. "There is no doubt the possibility of a war," he wrote, but he was not convinced that the slaughter would begin in the following months. He felt the British government – "as always, the pole of world politics" – would make further concessions to the Hitler regime in order to delay the outbreak of hostilities. Monte saw three signs for this:

1. The Polish question. During the summer, London and Warsaw had been squabbling over a loan that Poland needed to purchase weapons. The British government would only agree to the loan if the money were used to buy British arms, and the Polish negotiator scoffed at this condition. As a result, it did not seem that London would necessarily stand by its Polish ally in case of war.[32]

2. The Russian question. An English–French–Russian alliance had not yet materialized. The French were determined to form one, yet nothing had been signed because "the English are causing problems."

3. The Far Eastern question. The Japanese Empire wanted to force a "fundamental shift" in the Far East and expel British influence from China. Since mid-1937 hundreds of thousands of Japanese soldiers had been fighting against the Chinese republic, yet London was holding back.

From Monte's point of view, all of this was no coincidence. Newspapers around the world were reporting on the Hudson–Wohltat affair.

On July 20, Robert Hudson, the British Secretary for Overseas Trade, held a meeting with Germany's Export Minister Helmut Wohltat during a whaling conference in London. Hudson made a suggestion: If the Nazis were willing to stop their rearmament program, Great Britain could offer Germany a loan of perhaps one billion pounds. As these talks became public in the following days, there were contradictory statements and counter-statements in the press. Hudson explained that he had not spoken on behalf of his government – the British cabinet still entered into crisis. Even from today's perspective it is difficult to say exactly what happened behind the scenes.[33] For Monte, however, this was all just diplomatic spectacle: "Anyone who understands English politics – what am I saying – modern politics in general, knows that trial balloons like this are used as a first attempt to influence public opinion."

Monte saw these talks as a sign that the British government would continue its appeasement policy in order "to reach a better compromise with the Germans." The loan for Poland was in the same vein: Great Britain did not just want to "control the use of the lent money" but also force Poland to surrender the Danzig Corridor to the Germans. The British talks with the Soviet Union were based on deception: London was only negotiating with Moscow in order "to deceive the English public who sincerely desired an alliance with Russia after Hitler's march on Prague." The British people were opposed to Hitler, but Prime Minister Chamberlain was only interested in placating him. Monte wrote that British politics had "remained cautious and full of cunning."

This is how Monte came to write about the Soviet Union. He saw "a certain similarity" between England and Russia: "Yes, they both want peace [...] one to preserve its empire, its conquests of centuries [...]. And the other, Russia, wants peace to consolidate the gains of a new social order." The common ground between the two powers had been "created by the incessant aggressions of the fascist states." Nonetheless, the political distance between these temporary friends was "greater than the distance between London and Vladivostok, as great as the distance between the capitalist and the socialist order."

For British imperialism, Nazi Germany was an especially bellicose competitor – yet a competitor in the framework of the same social order. The Soviet Union, in contrast, had emerged from the October Revolution and represented an attempt to turn that entire order upside down. In Germany, the economy remained under the control of the capitalists – in Russia, capital had been expropriated.[34] That is why Chamberlain was reserved about an alliance with Stalin:

> Chamberlain does not want Hitler to fall, for he understands too well the danger that a proletarian dictatorship could be established in Germany. That is the danger that he and the whole English bourgeoisie fear. Which child could seriously doubt that a socialist Germany would be the beginning of the end of European capitalism?

Monte was developing an idea that he would present to German soldiers just a few years later: a new world war would lead to new socialist revolutions, just like the revolutionary wave that had shook the entire world at the end of the previous war. A German revolution could be the first link in the chain of world revolution. The Soviet Union represented a victory of the first revolutionary wave which could be expanded in the second. For this reason, the British bourgeoisie could not possibly be an ally of the Soviets.

Nonetheless, the Stalinist leadership of the Soviet Union and the Communist (Third) International relied on an alliance with the democratic imperialist countries, above all with Britain, against Nazi Germany. From 1935 onwards, the official communist parties in Spain, France and other countries formed "Popular Fronts" together with social democratic and bourgeois parties. These popular fronts were intended to stop the rise of fascism and prevent a war against the Soviet Union. To achieve this goal, the Stalinists had to convince their bourgeois allies that they had abandoned the goal of worldwide socialist revolution – in fact, the popular fronts explicitly guaranteed the defense of private property of the means of production. The German communists, for example, promised that after Hitler's fall they would work toward the establishment of a democratic, bourgeois and non-socialist republic in Germany.

In this same sense, the Comintern suddenly became pacifist. In 1920, the Comintern had resolved that each of its sections would "support – in deed, not merely in word – every colonial liberation movement."[35] The communist parties organized demonstrations and strikes against colonial rule, both in the metropole and in the periphery. By the second half of the 1930s, however, Stalin halted anti-colonial agitation in order to conciliate the democratic colonial powers England and France.[36] In an interview with an American journalist, Stalin went so far as to declare that fears about the Comintern's earlier plans for world revolution had been a "tragicomic misunderstanding."[37]

The process of "Stalinization" in the second half of the 1920s meant a break from the founding principles of the Communist International on diverse questions. The differentiation of the communist movement between the Stalinist leadership on the one hand and the Left Opposition (associated with the person of Leon Trotsky) on the other became public in 1927. At the time, the debate around Stalin's theory of "socialism in one country" seemed like an academic question: Could a socialist society be constructed in Russia if proletarian revolutions in the developed capitalist countries failed? Or were advances of the world revolution necessary for Russia to reach socialism? The party and state bureaucracy under Stalin, eager to defend its privileges, became more and more conservative in international politics. By 1930, all opposition had been purged from the communist parties – Stalin's word was law. The expelled Left Opposition founded the Fourth International in 1938.

By 1936, Stalinism and Trotskyism were on opposite sides of the barricades, and not just in a metaphorical sense. The Spanish Revolution broke out on July 19, 1936, when fascist generals attempted a coup and were beaten back by workers' mobilizations. The Bolshevik-Leninists (as Trotsky and his followers called themselves) fought for a workers' state based on councils – their strategy for Spain was modeled on the October Revolution in Russia. The Stalinists, on the other hand, maintained their political alliance with the anti-fascist parties of the bourgeoisie. During the revolution, workers occupied their factories and peasants collectivized the land. The Stalinists repressed these radical measures of the workers' movement in order to defend their bourgeois allies. The result of this policy was seen in the "May Days" in Barcelona in 1937, when Stalinism waged a civil war against revolutionary workers in the Catalan capital.[38]

Monte was developing an initial criticism of Stalin's strategy. Russian policy was intended to gain time, he wrote. But Hitler's annexation of Czechoslovakia gave German imperialism not only "new riches, more minerals, and further economic resources," but also "strategic positions that are primarily directed against Russia." Moreover, the "fascist order has great advantages as far as the preparations for war are concerned." In short, Hitler was in a better position than Stalin to use the time gained.

No less problematic was the fact that the bourgeois parties and governments remained suspicious of the Stalinists. For them, the Soviet state embodied a proletarian revolution – it remained, in Trotsky's words, a "degenerate workers' state" which the capitalist states could never accept. The biggest problem with Stalin's strategy was that it confused the working masses – the only force that could stop the war and overcome capitalism. Monte summarized the Stalinist "policy of compromise": "The formula [...] is that in this epoch, the proletariat of the different countries does not have the task of changing the social order, but rather of preventing armed aggression against the Soviet Union, forcing its own bourgeoisie to ally with Russia against the fascist threat."

In this formula, Monte recognized "a small mistake": It was the crisis of capitalism and the resulting intensification of the class struggle that was leading the bourgeoisie of all countries to bet on the fascist card. The trend toward fascism could be observed in the democratic countries of the West as well. That is why there was also "the danger of an attack against the Soviet Union by the democratic states." France or Great Britain could wage war against the workers' state, as they had already done in the years after the October Revolution. The only effective "bulwark of the Soviet Union," in Monte's eyes, was not an alliance with the French or British capitalists, but the mobilization of the international working class under an independent banner.

In this letter, Monte acknowledged his sympathies for Trotskyism for the first time more or less openly. For him, the impending war was not a struggle between "democracy" and "fascism" – it was an inner-imperialist conflict to redivide the world among the great powers.

In the end, in contrast to Monte's expectations, there was an alliance between the imperialist democracies and the Soviet Union. This was not just a result of the particular aggressiveness of German imperialism, but also because US capitalists recognized the opportunity to use the war to overtake Great Britain and conquer a hegemonic position in the imperialist world order. The imperialist character of the war became especially evident after the main fighting had ceased. The dust had not yet settled before the democratic colonial powers such as Great Britain, France, and the Netherlands started campaigns to put down uprisings in their colonies, with massacres in India, Algeria, Indonesia, Vietnam, etc. that cost hundreds of thousands of lives. After Germany's defeat, all capitalist powers quickly united in a Western alliance for the Cold War – an expression of the incompatibility of these two opposing social orders.

Monte had come full circle. A decade earlier, Paul Ehrlich had attempted to win him over to Trotskyism. Now Monte was attempting the same with his brother Carlo, who had just visited Ehrlich in the kibbutz. Carlo, however, was convinced of the need to differentiate between the two imperialist camps – democratic countries allied with the Soviet Union and fascist countries. Monte had nothing against such a differentiation, but he argued against the Third International's abandonment of the program of proletarian revolution. Monte had the uncompromising attitude of a recent convert: communists should not become part of any imperialist camp. (In the end, Monte could not convince his brother. Karl Monath joined the British Army in 1942, where he served as a lathe operator and an interpreter in Egypt and then in Italy.)[39]

On the last page of his letter, Monte switched back to German. He was pleased that he had been able to write in French "almost entirely without a dictionary." Still, there were "certainly many errors, especially in the use of idioms." Monte admitted in a footnote that he had his information on Trotskyism mostly from "the third," i.e. from the Comintern. From "the opposition," i.e. the Trotskyists, he had only read Trotsky's book *The Revolution Betrayed*. It may be that Monte was downplaying a budding acquaintance with the Trotskyists in Belgium, in the hope of convincing his younger brother. In any case we know that Monte had already read works by Trotsky a decade earlier, after receiving pamphlets from Ehrlich.

In this complicated political discussion about communist strategy in the face of the approaching war, misunderstandings and even "unnecessary bickering" were possible, Monte wrote. He felt the need to make some clarifications in his mother tongue. For example, he was "for the united front" just like his brother, but he was convinced that this was "not in contradiction to maintaining one's own program." In other words, Monte defended a united front of revolutionary and reformist workers' organizations for concrete demands. But he rejected the idea of abandoning opposition to imperialism and colonialism in order to form an anti-fascist alliance with bourgeois forces, as the Stalinists were doing with the popular front.[40]

At the end of the letter, Monte became nostalgic. He had "written away" the whole afternoon and planned to spend the evening alone in his room. He reminded his brother of the "historic day of [their] farewell." What was this farewell like? Why was Carlo deported to Poland but not Monte, even though both were Polish citizens living at the same address? We don't know – perhaps Monte avoided arrest, perhaps he was detained and then escaped, or perhaps he was being deported when the German authorities stopped the *Polenaktion* after three days. Monte remained in his room in Berlin for another six months. We only know his recollection of the last time he ever saw his brother, in October 1938. The two brothers were sitting together in a small German police station. "We are living in historic times," a detective told them. Monte recalled:

[We] were upset that world history again seemed determined to make our castles in the sky [...] collapse. [...] We have not exactly become despondent. And when I reflect about what came afterwards, for you and for me, then I wonder a little and shake my head philosophically. How much lies hidden in such a moment of human life? More, much more than in the blossom and the seed, with a devout beholder admiring the greatness of God (or nature).

A moment in human life is certainly a miracle, and the God of men is greater than the God of plants.[41]

In an addendum, Monte apologized for his handwriting. Anyone who could decipher his 18-page letter deserved to hang a "cuneiform medal" on his or her chest. (Comment by the author after many long and arduous hours of transcription: Apology accepted.)

4

Underground

4.1. *"I love Belgium": From Zionism to Trotskyism*

Abraham Wajnsztok, born in Warsaw in 1918, moved to Brussels
with his parents as a child. The family had previously emigrated to
Palestine, but returned to Poland before settling in Belgium.[1] While
still a teenager, Wajnsztok joined the socialist Zionist youth organization Hashomer Hatzair, and soon he was a leader of its Belgian section
and chairman of the Brussels federation. In 1936, he met the Trotskyist leader Walter Dauge – himself just shy of 30 – during a strike wave
in the mines of Wallonia. Like other members of Hashomer Hatzair
we have already encountered, Wajnsztok was quickly convinced of
Trotsky's positions. With a new approach to Marxism, he began to
study the Jewish question using the method of historical materialism.
He distributed his reflections within his organization in the form
of "theses on the Jewish question." These were later published as a
book: *The Jewish Question: A Marxist Interpretation.*[2]

Wajnsztok investigated why the Jewish people, after thousands
of years, still existed at all, while other Mediterranean peoples had
dissolved into different cultures. He found the answer not in the
Jewish religion or culture, but rather in the specific roles that Jews
had played in different class societies. They were discriminated
against, yet nonetheless fulfilled indispensable economic functions
– this was the basis of the internal cohesion of the Jewish people,
and also of their exclusion from each society. Wajnsztok examined
these different roles through the millennia. His conclusion was that
the modern antisemitism of the Nazis was a product of the decay of
capitalist society. That is why Zionism, attempting to build a Jewish
nation-state, could not offer a solution to the Jewish question: "An
evil cannot be suppressed without destroying its causes. But Zionism

wants to solve the Jewish question without destroying capitalism, which is the principal source of the suffering of the Jews."[3]

Wajnsztok, who now called himself Abraham Leon, had found a theoretical basis for a radical break with his Zionist past. In 1939, he and around 20 followers left Hashomer Hatzair to join the Revolutionary Socialist Party (PSR), the Belgian section of the Fourth International. After the German invasion in May of 1940, the PSR, which had already been devastated by faction fights, collapsed. Walter Dauge was arrested and abandoned the struggle. Leon played the leading role in rebuilding the section underground and was elected its political secretary. The organization, now called the Revolutionary Communist Party (PCR), published the illegal newspaper *La Voie de Lénine* (French: *Lenin's Course*).[4]

Leon's biography contains astonishing similarities to that of Monath. As sons of Polish Jewish immigrants in Western Europe, they grew up between two cultures. Their integration into Belgian and German societies was blocked by antisemitism, but they could not return to the Jewish culture of Eastern Europe. In Hashomer Hatzair, they searched for a new Jewish identity that broke with old traditions. In practice, however, the political project of Jewish socialism in Palestine proved to be a reactionary utopia. They recognized that socialism as a concrete response to the capitalist crisis could only be realized in an international context. The obvious choice for young Jewish revolutionaries would have been official communism. But the Stalin regime in the Soviet Union was displaying its antisemitic side. Leon became convinced of Trotskyism by the Moscow Trials of 1936, in which numerous leading Bolsheviks from the time of the October Revolution (many of them Jews) were executed for supposed sabotage.[5]

We are looking at Leon's biography because we know so little about Monath's time in Belgium. After his last (surviving) letter to his siblings from early August of 1939, everything happened very quickly. On August 23, Hitler and Stalin signed a non-aggression pact. The discussion about the advisability of an alliance between the Soviet Union and the democratic countries, which had led to disagreements between Monte and Carlo, was thus put on hold for the next two years. Until the German invasion of the Soviet Union in June 1941, the communist parties of the West denounced England and France as the main threats to peace – they remained silent about Hitler. Just a week after the Hitler–Stalin Pact, on September 1, the Wehrmacht invaded Poland – the Red Army followed on September 17. The Second World War had begun.

From this point on, Monte's life is a mystery. On May 10, 1940, the German army entered Belgium. Eighteen days later, the Belgian armed forces announced their unconditional surrender. One month after that, on June 22, the French army capitulated as well. We have just one sign of life from Monte from this time: On July 29, he sent a postcard to his siblings from south-western France (the French department of Pyrénées-Orientales, located on the Mediterranean coast and the Spanish border). Had Monte tried to flee Europe by ship? Had he marched in the long columns of refugees to the Free Zone in the south? We can only speculate. He merely wrote: "After long deliberations, and fully aware of all the possible consequences, I have decided to return to Belgium. [...] Sometimes I am a little bit afraid for you, but I think that despite the war in the Mediterranean we are in a reasonably safe milieu."[6]

This is the last message his siblings ever received from him. Monte was certainly not "reasonably safe." From the files of the Belgian Foreigners' Police we know he was officially registered as a refugee from May 1939 until at least 1942.[7] On the first page of his file there is a big stamp: "JUIF-JOOD"[8] – a particularly unfavorable status. He declared his citizenship as "Polish," but the authorities registered him as a stateless Jew. On August 20, 1939, Monte was threatened with deportation or imprisonment by the Foreigners' Police because he had not extended his residence permit. Somehow he was able to resolve the problem and remain in Belgium legally.

His asylum application asked why he had chosen Belgium as a destination (see Figure 7). He answered in French: "I love Belgium." He was more honest in a letter to his brother: As a Berliner, he found Brussels "interesting but small, and all the interesting things are soon depleted."[9] In realty, Belgium was the most accessible place for Jews from Germany – and Monte wanted to continue to France as quickly as possible.

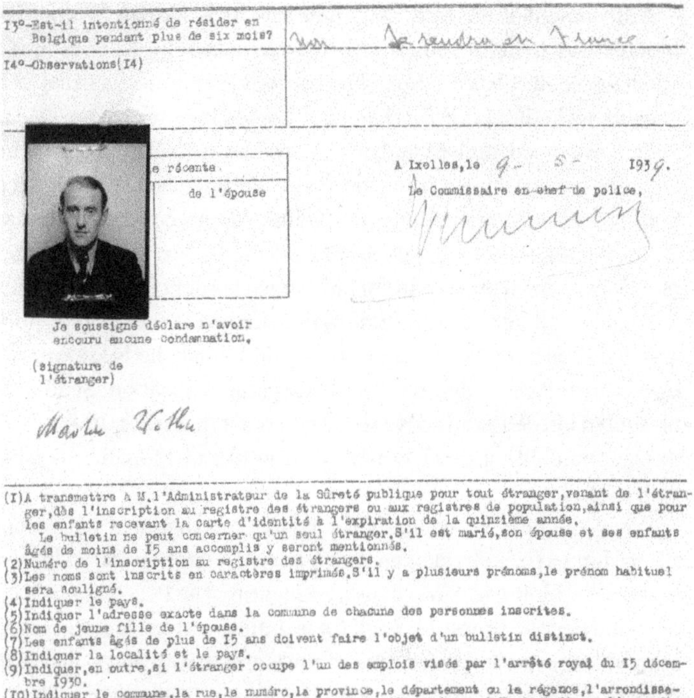

13°-Est-il intentionné de résider en Belgique pendant plus de six mois?

14°-Observations(14)

...e récente

de l'épouse

A Ixelles,le 9-5- 1939.

Le Commissaire en chef de police,

Je soussigné déclare n'avoir encouru aucune condamnation.

(signature de l'étranger)

(1)A transmettre à M.l'Administrateur de la Sûreté publique pour tout étranger,venant de l'étranger,dès l'inscription au registre des étrangers ou aux registres de population,ainsi que pour les enfants recevant la carte d'identité à l'expiration de la quinzième année.
Le bulletin ne peut concerner qu'un seul étranger.S'il est marié,son épouse et ses enfants âgés de moins de 15 ans accomplis y seront mentionnés.
(2)Numéro de l'inscription au registre des étrangers.
(3)Les noms sont inscrits en caractères imprimés.S'il y a plusieurs prénoms,le prénom habituel sera souligné.
(4)Indiquer le pays.
(5)Indiquer l'adresse exacte dans la commune de chacune des personnes inscrites.
(6)Nom de jeune fille de l'épouse.
(7)Les enfants âgés de plus de 15 ans doivent faire l'objet d'un bulletin distinct.
(8)Indiquer la localité et le pays.
(9)Indiquer,en outre,si l'étranger occupe l'un des emplois visés par l'arrêté royal du 15 décembre 1930.
(10)Indiquer le commune,la rue,le numéro,la province,le département ou la régence,l'arrondissement,le cercle ou le canton et le pays.S'il s'agit d'une adresse à Paris,indiquer l'arrondissement.
(11)Indiquer les communes,la rue,le numéro,les dates d'arrivée et de départ dans chaque commune.
(12)Indiquer:a)la nature des papiers que l'étranger produit pour justifier son identité,les lieu et date de leur délivrance,l'autorité qui les a délivrés; b)s'il s'agit d'un passeport,indiquer,en outre,la durée de validité; c)éventuellement,mentionner les date et lieu de délivrance et la durée de validité du visa consulaire belge; d)éventuellement,indiquer les conditions restrictives de séjour en Belgique inscrites sur ce visa; e)indiquer si l'étranger est détenteur du permis d'entrée prévu par l'arrêté royal du 15 décembre 1930(main-d'oeuvre étrangère); f)ne transmettre les papiers que dans le cas où il existerait des doutes sur leur authenticité ou leur applicabilité au porteur.
(13)Indiquer le motif.
(14)Indiquer si l'étranger a été invité à quitter le pays ou si le certificat d'inscription n'a pas été délivré ou si la carte d'identité a été délivrée dès l'inscription.Mentionner les raisons qui s'opposeraient au séjour en Belgique.
(15)En cas d'impossibilité,dactyloscoper un autre doigt et indiquer celui-ci.Faire mention du refus éventuel de l'étranger de se soumettre à cette formalité.

Empreinte roulée de l'index droit(15)	
du mari	de l'épouse

habite à l'adresse
Ixelles le 6-5-39
le Com.-adjoint,

Figure 7 From Monath's application for asylum in Belgium in May 1939. From the State Archives of Belgium.

A document from April 24, 1940 says that Martin Witlin (i.e. Monte) was living together with the German refugee Fritz Sidlof at Chaussée de Vleurgat No. 15 in Brussels.[10] Witlin was listed as a student at the *Institut Polytechnique* at Rue de Londres No. 11. "He is known as a good student and attends classes regularly." Witlin's file includes a short notice from the Police President of Berlin stating that he had no criminal record.[11] Sidlof's file, in contrast, contains a similar letter from the Police President of Vienna. This letter mentions a conviction for an "unauthorized border crossing" into the Saarland and summarizes: "[Sidlof] is described as reluctant to work and does not have a good reputation. Additionally he is known as a Communist Party supporter."[12] In his asylum application, Sidlof had presented himself as an active social democrat in Austria. In any case, the German authorities had not taken notice of Monath's socialist convictions.

When the Belgian section of the Fourth International was reconstituted in 1940, a German emigrant named Viktor appeared for the first time – Monte had found his new identity. The PCR was made up of young people. Ernest Mandel, for example, was ten years younger than Viktor – just 17 at the time of the German invasion – but soon became a leading figure of Belgian Trotskyism. In an interview with Rodolphe Prager in 1977, Mandel shared his recollections of Viktor:

[He] was with us since the reconstruction of the Belgian organization in August/September of 1940. From the beginning he was a member of the leadership. I only saw him at CC [Central Committee] meetings so I don't know the details of his activities. The only personal memory I have is from my first trip to Paris, which I took together with him in November or December of 1943, about two months before the European Conference. This is the only time I was in Viktor's company for an extended time. His boldness made a big impression on me; this enabled him to escape from dangerous situations. He was not a Jewish type, and he appeared at ease with German soldiers. He was very German in appearance and mentality. He already had lots of practice in illegality.[13]

How did Monte take his final steps toward Trotskyism and become Viktor? His development must have been similar to that of Leon. Like Leon, Monte expressed disgust at the Moscow Trials. He had read a book by Lion Feuchtwanger, the "court poet of the Kremlin," which he found "downright ghastly": Feuchtwanger "attempts to explain away the illogical parts [of the trials] with an Eastern mentality that one simply cannot understand in the West." Monte recalled that the Bolshevik leaders, "their books and speeches and deeds," had "always been completely comprehensible for us in the West" – but perhaps Feuchtwanger had never understood them in the first place.[14]

In contrast to Leon, however, Monte had left Hashomer Hatzair as an individual and spent several years abstaining from politics. Leon, who had elaborated a theoretical alternative to socialist Zionism, must have recruited the emigrant Monte, five years his senior, to the ranks of the Fourth International.[15] The dead end of Zionism had become apparent to many – not just in the kibbutzim in Palestine. The urgent question was how to fight against the Nazis. In the absence of concrete information from Belgium, we will look to New York for an illustration of how Hashomer Hatzair and the Fourth International competed directly and publicly for the hearts of young Jewish socialists.

4.2. *"The fight against fascism is here and now": Nazis in New York*

On February 20, 1939, the German American Bund, a pro-Nazi organization in the US, held a rally in New York's Madison Square Garden. Jewish people made up almost 30 percent of the city's population. Yet no Jewish organizations called for protests against the Nazis. Two Yiddish-language newspapers advised their readers to steer clear of the area around the garden. The American Jewish Committee even supported the Nazi's right to free speech.[16]

Only the Trotskyists of the American Socialist Workers Party (SWP) mobilized against the fascist Bund. In the run-up to the counter-demonstration, a delegation of the "Yipsels" (as the SWP's youth organization, the YPSL, was called) visited the offices of Hashomer Hatzair on the Lower East Side. There they were told: "Sorry, but we can't join you. Our Zionist policy is to take no part in politics outside

Palestine." The SWP responded with an appeal in its newspaper (*Socialist Appeal*, edited by Max Shachtman) for "An End To Zionist Illusions!" It called Zionism a "criminal waste" of the "energies and minds and hearts of millions of Jewish men and women and boys and girls – not to speak of the hundreds of millions of dollars it took." The Trotskyists declared:

> It is an immediate task of our party to get those boys and girls out on the picket line with us next time, to awaken the Jewish people to the realization that the fight against anti-Semitism, which is the fight against fascism, is here and now, and all the real fighters against fascism belong in the ranks of the Socialist Workers Party![17]

On February 20, up to 22,000 people came to the Nazi rally. Under US and Swastika flags, *Bundesführer* Fritz Kuhn ranted against "Frank D. Rosenfeld" and his "Jew Deal," part of a Judeo-Bolshevik conspiracy. On the stage, guards in SA-style uniforms stood at attention in front of a huge portrait of George Washington.[18] Outside the arena, however, 50,000 to 80,000 antifascists had gathered. Most of them were Jews, but there were also supporters of the black nationalist Marcus Garvey and rank-and-file members of the Communist Party. Street battles raged outside the garden for five hours. Only the mounted police could protect the Nazi rally. This protest had been organized by the New York Trotskyists.[19]

This scene illustrates the political contrast between Zionism and Trotskyism. The extermination of the European Jews had already begun. Zionism, even in its most left-wing variant, only had one answer: *aliyah* (emigration to Palestine). Yet due to the restrictions of the British colonial authorities, emigration was slowed to a trickle. For the millions of Jews who were persecuted and directly threatened by German fascism, Palestine was not an option. What to do? Herschel Grynszpan was not alone. Jewish young people all over the world were aching to fight against Hitler. The Fourth International offered them an international structure and above all a political program. This offer was accepted in Brussels, Haifa, and New York.[20]

4.3. *"This is not our war": Member of the Fourth International*

The Fourth International had been founded for war.[21] Trotsky and his supporters, despite their meager forces, were committed to raising the banner of revolutionary internationalism as high as possible before a new imperialist slaughter broke out. They were determined to avoid a repetition of the terrible disorientation in the workers' ranks at the beginning of the First World War, when barely a voice against the war could be heard.

Yet the Fourth International, already weak, was shaken as the war approached. Leading members including Max Shachtman and C.L.R. James broke with the International because they no longer supported the characterization of the Soviet Union as a "degenerated workers' state." For Trotsky, the fundamental social order that had emerged from the October Revolution, despite the tremendous bureaucratic deformation, remained basically intact. The groups that split away, in contrast, believed that the Soviet Union under Stalin had mutated into a new kind of class society with imperialist policies. Due to this split, the International Executive Committee ceased to function. An emergency conference of the Fourth International with delegates from ten sections met in New York from May 19–26, 1940. It passed a "Manifesto on Imperialist War and the Proletarian Revolution," drafted by Trotsky, which closed with the call: "This is not our war!"

> In contradistinction to the Second and Third Internationals, the Fourth International builds its policy not on the military fortunes of the capitalist states but on the transformation of the imperialist war into a war of the workers against the capitalists.[22]

The conference elected a new International Secretariat based in New York. But a number of sections in Europe were cut off from the New York leadership and from each other.

The German section of the Fourth International, the International Communists of Germany (IKD), was particularly devastated. At the conference it was reported that of the IKD's 1,000 members, roughly half had withdrawn in 1933, while 150 were in prisons and concentration camps.[23] The section's leadership in exile, the Foreign Committee (AK) under Josef Weber (known by his pseudonym Johre), was able to escape to Paris and then in 1940 to New York. But these leaders were distancing themselves from the strategic goal of socialist revolution – in light of fascist barbarism, they came to believe a new bourgeois enlightenment was necessary. By the end of the war, the AK of the IKD had completely broken with Marxism.[24] Only small, scattered IKD groups continued Trotskyist activities, and they were largely cut off from each other.[25]

Re-establishing the links between the sections of the Fourth International involved considerable danger. In January of 1942, the French section sent a delegation including Marcel Hic and Yvan Craipeau to Brussels for a meeting with the Belgian section. Later, a meeting in the Belgian Ardennes founded a European Secretariat – it remains unclear who was in attendance at this meeting. This new body organized political discussions among the Trotskyist groups in Europe – the national question under the Nazi occupation in particular led to heated debates. The secretariat was based in Paris and in practice was run by just one person: Marcel Hic.[26]

A truly collective leadership body emerged only after a six-day conference in July of 1943 in Paris. Delegates from France, Belgium, Spain, Greece, and Germany elected a Provisional European Secretariat. Its members were Michel Raptis (Pablo), Marcel Hic and Nicolas Spoulber (Marcoux) from the French section, and Leon-Wajnsztok from the Belgian section. Monat-Widelin was also a member and responsible for the "German work." A report of this conference in a US Trotskyist magazine provides yet another name for Viktor: Wintley.[27] Viktor, already a leading member of the Belgian section, was now assuming tasks in the international leadership. The French Trotskyists requested a native speaker to lead the Trotskyist work of subverting the German army there. For this task, Viktor moved to Paris in May 1943.[28] Together with other German emigrants in Paris, he founded a "League of Communist-Internationalists (German Section of the Fourth International)." There is not much evidence of this small group's activity – except for the newspaper *Arbeiter und Soldat*.[29]

4.4. *"The main enemy is at home": Revolutionary Defeatism*

"The main enemy is at home!" This slogan appeared on a leaflet written by Karl Liebknecht during the First World War, and it soon became a catchphrase for the revolutionary opposition to imperialist war.[30] Liebknecht's position was adopted by the Communist International, which coined the term "revolutionary defeatism." This meant calling for the defeat of one's own government in an imperialist war, without desiring the victory of the other side. Instead, the workers' movement should reject any kind of *Burgfrieden* (German: civic peace or class truce) and intensify the class struggle during wartime, regardless of the consequences for the military situation. Would that not aid the enemy? That is what the ruling classes and their reformist agents claimed, since they needed a quiet hinterland to conduct their wars. The experiences at the end of the First World War, however, had shown that revolutionary victories on one side of the front would quickly lead to further uprisings in the ranks of the opposing armies. The goal of "defeatism" was an international proletarian revolution that would overthrow all capitalist governments.

Revolutionary defeatism was a principle of the Communist International at the time of its foundation. But Stalinism had thrown this principle to the wind, along with so many others. By the second half of the 1930s, the communists loyal to Moscow offered unreserved support for every bourgeois government that was allied with the Soviet Union. When the war broke out, Stalin was allied with Hitler. Accordingly, the Stalinist press praised the *Führer* as a defender of peace. Only after Operation Barbarossa, the Nazis' surprise invasion of the Soviet Union in June 1941, did the official communist parties switch their allegiances to the Allied governments. Only the Fourth International maintained Lenin's policy of defeatism. The Trotskyists refused to support any imperialist government, even if it was at war with Hitler. German fascism was to be overthrown by a revolutionary uprising of the masses – and for this, it was necessary to advance the class struggle in the countries threatened or occupied by Germany, while remaining independent of all wings of the bourgeoisie.[31]

The reader will ask: Was this not a dangerous illusion? Could revolutionary workers really bring down the Nazi regime? Indeed, there was relatively little proletarian resistance within Germany, and this was not just a result of the murderous repression – the Allied bombing campaign was also conceived to prevent the development of an independent movement of the German population against Hitler.[32] For the fascist rulers, the danger of revolution was imminently present. Hitler and his lieutenants had been profoundly affected by the collapse of the German Reich in 1918. In a conversation shortly before the outbreak of the war, when Hitler was still attempting to present himself as a friend of peace, the French ambassador Robert Coulondre warned him: "Though I was [...] definitely certain of our victory, I feared, at the same time, that at the end of a war, the sole real victor would be M. Trotsky."[33] Of course the diplomat did not mean that Trotsky would return from exile and lead a new Soviet government in Europe. Instead, Trotsky's name had become synonymous with an independent revolutionary policy of the proletariat. The European Trotskyists intended to make the nightmare of the French and German governments a reality.

Armed with this strategic conception, the French Trotskyists attempted to organize fraternization between the German occupation soldiers and the French workers. The Stalinists, in contrast, rejected such a policy. They assumed that the German soldier was so steadfastly obedient that he would only break with the Hitler regime if his officers did so first. For this reason they founded a "National Committee for a Free Germany" (NKFD) and a "League of German Officers" (BDO) with a thoroughly bourgeois program tailored to the Wehrmacht generals. The Stalinists renounced any socialist objectives – the "free" Germany they called for was to be led by monarchist officers. The NKFD even rejected the German republican colors, black-red-gold – the committee instead used the old imperial (and Nazi) colors, black-white-red.[34] Stalin spoke of a "great patriotic war," i.e. a conflict between nations and not between classes. After Hitler broke the alliance with Stalin, the French Communist Party (PCF) became patriotic and used the slogan: "Everyone united against the *Boches!*"[35] This was a jingoistic term for Germans that had been used during the First World War in particular.

The Trotskyists worked with the opposite hypothesis: Despite their fanatical education, the majority of the German soldiers were young men from the working class. Despite all the repression, communist, social democratic, and trade union traditions continued to exist underground. One could address the soldiers directly and incite them against their aristocratic and fascist officers – even more so as it became increasingly obvious that an Axis victory was impossible. This is why the Trotskyists opposed all forms of anti-German chauvinism. They remained loyal to Lenin's position from the First World War: The cause of war was not to be found in the particular barbarism of this or that nation, but rather in the contradictions of the imperialist system. Consequently, only the socialist revolution – through the combined efforts of working people of all nations – could end the war. The Trotskyist newspaper *La Verité* replied to the PCF in 1942: "All united, German and French, against the Nazis! All united against the chauvinists of every color, the worst enemies of the working class!"[36]

The Trotskyists' practical goal was the fraternization of workers and soldiers on both sides. Many factors made this work extremely difficult: The historical rivalry between the French and the Germans, the obscurantist ideology propagated within the Wehrmacht, the day-to-day brutality of the occupation, and especially the terrible repression by the Gestapo and their helpers from the French Milice, the political paramilitary force of the collaborationist Vichy regime. The Stalinist and bourgeois partisans focused on assassinations of so-called "boches." The American Trotskyist George Breitman, however, explained why fraternization was the most effective form of resistance:

It was far easier to stick a knife between the ribs of a German soldier on a dark night than to meet that same German in the daytime, win his confidence and enlist him in the ranks of the revolutionary fighters against fascism. But difficult though this work was, Widelin [i.e. Viktor] carried it out with growing success.[37]

4.5. "We fight against capitalism": Cells in the German Army

How was fraternization possible? The beginnings of this work remain largely in the dark. Many of the protagonists did not survive the war.

Recollections are scattered across different autobiographies and are often contradictory. One individual, however, stands out: Robert Cruau, a 23-year-old postal worker (see Figure 8). In April 1943, Cruau moved to Brest together with the Berthomé brothers, Georges and Henri. They had fled Nantes to escape the forced labor program of the German occupiers, the *Service du Travail Obligatoire*. They joined the local group of the Internationalist Workers Party (POI). As fellow POI member André Calvès later recalled: "Robert is bursting with activity. This is often the case when one begins to act outside the law."[38] Cruau spoke German and wanted to intensify the propaganda among the soldiers:

> [He] manages to get to know a sergeant whose father had been a communist functionary. The sergeant is already fairly politicized. He has access to certain official stamps and can provide various services to different friends. [...] Soon a small group of German soldiers is editing a bulletin and we print a hundred copies: *Arbeiter im Westen* [*Worker in the West*]. According to Robert, the bulletin has a very direct influence on 27 soldiers and sailors.[39]

At the massive naval base in Brest, German troops were stationed in one place for months at a time – an essential condition for the conspiratorial work of persuasion.[40] Hundreds of French workers were ordered to perform forced labor to construct the U-boat bunker. One of the first soldiers Cruau established contact with belonged to a "DCA," an anti-aircraft unit.[41]

Soon the Brest Trotskyists were helping a small group of German soldiers produce their own small newspaper. What was the name of the publication? Different names are given: Calvès recalled *Arbeiter im Westen*, while *La Verité* quoted from *Der Arbeiter*. Small scraps have been preserved from a *Zeitung für Soldat und Arbeiter im Westen* (*Newspaper for Soldier and Worker in the West*) (see Figure 9). This awkward name is the correct one. Issue "No. 2" from the summer of 1943 contains the slogan: "Long live the worker!" *La Verité* quoted from it in mid-October, after the group had been smashed. The newspaper was written with a typewriter and contained primitive sketches. On one side, we see a happy farmer sowing seeds next to a

Figure 8   Trotskyist postal worker
Robert Cruau (c.1940).
Photographer unknown, from Critique
communiste, No. 25, November 1978.

factory – on the other, a clique of Nazis and capitalists have banknotes
flying around their heads.

These scraps give the impression of a newspaper written by
recently politicized German soldiers and not by Trotskyist cadres.
La Verité quoted from "*Der Arbeiter*, Organ of the German soldiers'
committees':

> We, soldiers, finding ourselves in enemy countries, are in truth
> nothing but workers, proletarians, who must carry out the orders
> of the Nazi dictatorship. The situation of our comrades back home
> is little better [...]. We, like them, have to flog our guts out, always
> for nothing. Will we get the slightest benefit from this? No! So why
> all this? Will we keep going with this pointless war? No, and once
> again no. I have always behaved as a good German and obeyed my
> superiors' orders, but now, enough. Why continue this war which
> cannot possibly lead to any result?[42]

Figure 9   *The Newspaper for Soldier and Worker in the West,*
produced by German soldiers in Brest in summer 1943.

The newspaper called for "a socialist council republic" to provide peace, jobs and bread for all. It concluded with the slogan from the end of the *Communist Manifesto*: "Proletarians of all countries, unite!"

The French Trotskyists supported this work, but the political responsibility lay with the German soldiers themselves. Thus, *La Verité* even offered criticisms of the soldiers:

Der Arbeiter calls on German soldiers to join the revolutionary struggle. It says: "Drop your weapons and join the Fourth International." This slogan is not correct, since the point is not that they should drop their weapons, but rather that they should direct them against their class enemies. However this is just a mistaken turn of phrase, of no consequence. The young soldier who raises his head from the ranks has not yet found the correct "formula." If he has dropped his weapon, he will soon enough pick it up again, for the revolution: for his whole outlook is profoundly revolutionary.[43]

The Stalinists also made propaganda in German – but their goal was for Wehrmacht soldiers to voluntarily surrender and become prisoners of war. The Trotskyists, in contrast, wanted to turn the soldiers into political subjects and fighters for the socialist revolution – just as the soldiers at the end of the First World War had been at the forefront of revolutionary movements in a number of countries. The Trotskyists' hypothesis was confirmed by the formation of the Brest group. Trotskyism was able to attract soldiers who desired a quick end to the war, yet still did not have a strong grasp of the principles of the Fourth International or of communism in general.

This becomes clear when we look at the remaining scraps of the *Zeitung für Soldat und Arbeiter im Westen*. This newspaper contained impeccable internationalist slogans, such as "the liquidation of fascism through the liquidation of capitalism." But in correspondences, the common soldiers described their own motivations for joining the Fourth International. One anonymous German soldier reported from his time on leave: "My hometown has been completely destroyed." Most houses had been bombed, prices had increased tenfold, and the situation was "catastrophic." Another interesting observation by this soldier: "Our women and girls have been utterly debauched by the many foreign workers." We are dealing with a soldier whose head is still full of all kinds of chauvinistic prejudices – he simply could not stand the war for one more second. Thus, he ended up with the most radical faction in the Second World War. "The way has been shown to me by the IV International, where you can also help out and contribute to ending the war as quickly as possible."[44] This simple language will be familiar to any activist who reads workplace bulletins: One recognizes a recently politicized person who will develop quickly via further discussions with his new communist friends. At first, however, we see nothing more than a soldier's burning desire to end the war before it killed him.

Another letter sounds almost identical. "A fellow soldier"[45] reported about the letters full of lamentations from his family back home. He couldn't "stand it anymore." In similarly plain language, he appealed to other soldiers: "I am therefore in favor of putting an end to this abhorrent war. After all, we soldiers can do something for this first and foremost. I know a sure way which is also the right one for you. I cannot do anything on my own, so you have to help and collaborate." He thought of himself as a member of the Fourth International – which he almost certainly was not at this point – and explained his political logic: "We fight against capitalism and for the fraternization of the whole world. With this goal we make it impossible for any state to rule or dictate over Germany in the future, or that it is partitioned among other countries."[46] This soldier was equally incapable of formulating his political goals without chauvinist prejudices – he was primarily concerned with Germany's sovereignty at the end of the war (very different than the Fourth International's program for the United Socialist States of Europe). The soldier wanted no one to "fear a worse life" at the war's end. He ended with a call that one seldom reads in Trotskyist publications: "Think of your wives and [children]."[47]

This newspaper was typeset by André Calvès – who could not read German. "I have not forgotten the drudgery of typing a stencil in a language one does not understand." Calvès printed in a workshop hidden beneath his garden. A small hole led to an underground room with concrete walls and a reinforced roof, illuminated by a light bulb. "Of course one has to be young to get into the hiding place." It was built by Calvès and his brother, the only ones who knew it, "and it was never discovered."[48]

The fraternization work was slowly taking off – a project of very young German soldiers and equally young French workers. Viktor, now a leading member of the Fourth International and also a native German speaker, had been called on to centralize and lead this work politically. He threw himself at this task with all his energy. But, as Trotsky said, "man does not live from politics alone."[49] First Viktor needed a place to stay.

4.6. *"Literature hidden in the basement": At Home with the Thalmanns*

The large house in Paris' 14th arrondissement had a wonderful library:

> There was just about everything: Paul Frölich's collection of several hundred volumes on the French Revolution, the most important socialist classics, Lenin's collected works, almost all of Trotsky's writings, German and French fiction, books on the history of the revolutionary movement and the Russian Revolution.[50]

Viktor was now living illegally in France. Yet he could still read books avidly, just like when he was a schoolboy in the Berlin City Library. The house's library was illegal as well:

> All this more or less compromising literature was hidden in the basement, while the bookcases in the large room on the ground floor were filled with Chinese literature that a friend of ours, a Hungarian sinologist, had placed there for safekeeping; the Chinese books served as protection against any unwelcome visitors.[51]

This "pavilion" with seven rooms on the Rue Friant in the southern part of Paris had belonged to a Russian Jew who had fled to Lyon. He asked the Swiss German couple Paul and Clara Thalmann to move in, without paying rent, so the occupation authorities would not notice the house was empty and confiscate it. In May of 1943, Viktor joined them and remained until October. The Thalmanns also housed other revolutionary emigrants.[52]

These new housemates were not a perfect political fit. Paul Thalmann had been a leading member of the Communist Party of Switzerland, representing its youth wing at two congresses of the Comintern, before being expelled in 1929 for his criticism of Stalinism. After that, he was active in the Communist Party Opposition (KPO), associated with the right-wing opposition in the Comintern and especially with the German KPO under Heinrich

Brandler and August Thalheimer. Thalmann left the KPO in 1934 and helped to build the Trotskyist group "Marxist Action." In 1936, he and his wife Clara went to Spain to fight in the anti-fascist militias against Franco's troops. After the "May Days" in Barcelona, both were imprisoned by the Stalinist secret service, but were released after a few weeks. They fled to France, where they maintained contacts with the Trotskyists, but also with anarchists and left communists. Thalmann distanced himself from Trotsky's analysis of the Soviet Union as a "degenerate workers' state" – he believed that "Soviet imperialism" had become almost indistinguishable from the imperialist powers. Therefore, Thalmann rejected any critical defense of the Soviet Union in the Second World War. He broke with the Fourth International and founded a "Union of International Communists" together with emigrants from different countries, with a vague program against fascism and Bolshevism. He saw the Soviet Union as a "new imperialist state which, on the basis of the nationalization of the means of production, has created a new order that is neither socialist nor classically capitalist."[53]

In his autobiography, Thalmann claimed that the Parisian Trotskyists had been unable to find Viktor a place to live.[54] That is how Thalmann and Viktor ended up sharing a house, despite their major theoretical differences: "I had dreadful arguments with Viktor. Our views on Russia were far apart. He stuck to the old template of a 'degenerate workers' state'. Nevertheless, we got along well."[55]

Even under the name Viktor, Monte remained true to himself. In occupied Paris he attended concerts to listen to classical music. Thalmann reproached him for sitting in an audience full of Nazi officers. "I don't see them at all," Viktor countered. "I only hear Beethoven."[56]

The large house contained not only a library, but also a hand-operated duplicator and half a dozen typewriters – primitive printing equipment, but enough to produce a hectographed newspaper. After long discussions, Thalmann and Viktor decided to publish a newspaper for German soldiers – one that would deliberately exclude the Russian question. "Nothing fundamental about Russia, everything against Hitler, criticism of the Allies, but only in a secondary position."[57] The first number appeared in July of 1943. The ten hectographed pages were not intended for agitation – there were already leaflets for that. Instead, the newspaper served as a basis for discussing questions of strategy and theory with Wehrmacht soldiers who had already been drawn in via fliers and conversations.

4.7. *"The German Revolution is World Revolution"*: Arbeiter und Soldat

By the summer of 1943, it had become obvious that the Axis powers could not win the war. The German defeat in Stalingrad on February 2 marked the turning point. The Allies were advancing in North Africa and preparing for the invasion of Sicily. In the Pacific, the Japanese military was forced to abandon one island after another. Resistance was growing inside the fascist territories as well. The partisan movements in Yugoslavia and Greece liberated ever larger areas while similar movements expanded in France and Italy. On April 19, the Warsaw Ghetto Uprising began, and the German army needed a full month to put it down. These setbacks for the fascist governments led to tensions within the ruling classes. The same forces that had once played the fascist card in order to crush the workers' movement now tried to distance themselves from the increasingly unpopular leaders. On July 24, Italy's Great Fascist Council voted to depose Mussolini. He was arrested and liberated by German paratroopers 45 days later.[58] All German soldiers must have wondered what Germany's approaching defeat would look like. What would it mean for them and their families? Would there be a dictated peace that would eclipse the Treaty of Versailles? Would Germany be partitioned?

The first issue of *Arbeiter und Soldat*, dated July 1943, looks inconspicuous: Ten pages written on a typewriter, underneath a hand-drawn logo. Above the logo there is a quote from Karl Liebknecht: "The German revolution is world revolution."[59] The first sentence reveals the publishers' insurrectionary intentions: "Once again the specter of the communist revolution is haunting the world." Even though the authors remained anonymous, Monte's invincible optimism is hard to miss. The publication's name was inspired by the Bolshevik paper *Rabochii i Soldat*, which first appeared in Petrograd on July 23, 1917, after Kerensky's Provisional Government had banned *Pravda*.[60] The name *Worker and Soldier* was a signal: Even though repression might have the upper hand for the moment, the editors were preparing for the coming insurrection.

Viktor strived to make the Trotskyist program comprehensible to newly politicized young soldiers. Over ten pages, he presented lessons from the history of the workers' movement – which is always the basis of Marxist theory.[61] Viktor wrote about the German Revolution of 1918–19, the Russian Revolution of 1917, the Spanish Revolution of 1936–9, and the conclusions that could be drawn from each. Again and again he stressed the need for a revolutionary communist party, while arguing that the official communist parties under Stalin's leadership had ceased to be revolutionary. To support this claim, the first issue contained an article on the dissolution of the Third International on June 10, 1943, which was essentially a summary of the "Manifesto on the Dissolution of the Comintern" drafted by Marcel Hic.[62] This self-liquidation had come as a surprise to many officials and members of the communist parties, who were eager to interpret it as a maneuver. For the Trotskyists, however, this only confirmed that Stalin had sacrificed the world revolution on the altar of his alliance with the democratic imperialist powers. In addition to a few shorter articles, the issue concluded with Lenin's slogan from 1917: "Peace! Freedom! Bread!" The next two issues of August and September were in the same format, albeit somewhat shorter. They also included letters from soldiers. We will refrain from providing quotes and summaries here – the complete text can be found in Part II.

Viktor was the driving force behind the editorial work. It is hard to say who else contributed. Thalmann claimed that he and Viktor alternated writing all the articles. Viktor, however, alone led the discussion circles with the soldiers in Brest, using the newspaper as a basis: "Once or twice a week, Viktor made the dangerous journey to Brest; there he met German soldiers at night, discussed with them, received letters and short articles."[63] We can picture these meetings as insanely risky Marxist history lessons. The electrician Roland Filiâtre, a member of the Trotskyist organization in Paris, explained how the newspaper made its way across Europe:

The French comrades initiated discussions with German soldiers and got them talking and giving hints of their past politics. Once they had shown themselves trustworthy, after screening they were put in touch with the German soldiers who produced *Der Arbeiter* and then taken care of by their organization. The Paris region was organized as two branches. But the heart of the organization was in Brittany, both around Nantes and in particular around Brest where the soldiers provided the party with *Ausweis* [identity cards] and weapons. In Brest the organization had about 50 soldiers on average despite some people being posted elsewhere. Contacts were established in Toulon, Valence, La Rochelle and at Conches aerodrome. There was also an organization in Belgium. Links were established with the German Trotskyist organization, most importantly in the port of Hamburg, in Lübeck and in Rostock. Victor was responsible for these contacts. *Arbeiter und Soldat* was also distributed in garrisons in Italy."[64]

Filiâtre's recollections, however, are almost certainly exaggerated. Calvès directly contradicted some of his claims. Did the soldiers provide identity cards and weapons to the Trotskyist party POI? Calvès, who was familiar with this work first hand, answered: "Identity cards yes, weapons no." Even though the newspaper was distributed across France, "the only corresponding organization, founded by young fighters, was in Brest."[65] It is not clear if there were any connections to Germany. There is certainly no other evidence of Trotskyist groups in Hamburg, Lübeck, or Rostock that were still active in 1943.

5

The End

5.1. "Nothing will stop us": The Gestapo Strikes

On October 6, 1943, André Calvès took the train from Paris to his hometown of Brest. It was supposed to arrive at eight o'clock in the morning, but only entered the station around eleven. In Paris, Calvès had heard talk of an "incident" in Brest, but no one knew any details. When he stepped onto the platform, he met two German soldiers he knew from the underground meetings. One of them was Konrad Leplow from Hamburg. "[K]onrad seems surprised," Calvès recalled, "but I only notice that later." Konrad said that everything was in order and proposed to meet at two o'clock in the afternoon at the house of fellow Trotskyist André Darley. Calvès said goodbye in his broken German and went to a cooperative. There he met Micheline Trévien, wife of POI member Gérard Trévien. She hugged him and wept: "Gérard was arrested, along with many other comrades." Robert Cruau had already been shot – it was unclear if he had attempted to escape or the Gestapo merely claimed this. Then came even worse news: "[K]onrad betrayed us. He was present at the raids." The police had planned an ambush at Darley's house, where Trévien had been arrested. Calvès was able to escape Brest by train to Kerhuon and then to Paris.[1]

A German search party went to Calvès' house in Brest where they ran into his little brother Gérard. The officer said that André had done "bad things." Gérard, who also took part in the conspiratorial work, confirmed that André was the "madman of the house." The German officer replied that he knew that the two brothers did not get along. The search party threatened to dig up the entire garden, but it was a thousand square meters, and in the end the Germans left without any spoils. The underground printing workshop remained hidden until the end of the war. Gérard was spared.

Why did the Germans think that André and Gérard were at odds with each other? Only when the two brothers met up in a hiding place at the end of 1943 were they able to solve this mystery. André had met up with Konrad a month before the arrests to hand over some leaflets. That day, André had borrowed a shirt from his little brother, and Gérard had complained: "I am the only one in this house who takes care of clothes!" At the meeting, Konrad talked about his wife, who was living in constant fear in Hamburg. Then he asked about Calvès' family. André replied moodily that his brother was not interested in anything but shirts. This small misunderstanding might well have saved Gérard from deportation. It also shows that Leplow collaborated with the Gestapo well before the raids.

In his memoirs, Calvès admitted that the young soldiers in the cells – inspired by their initial successes – became overconfident: "the compartmentalization [of the organization] is not sufficiently ensured. Once, Robert met with ten soldiers at the house of a female friend who had just recently been recruited [...]. Ten soldiers together! It was madness. Nobody said it. We believed, without thinking, that everything would be ok."[2] Nevertheless, Calvès rejected the idea that the organization had been destroyed because of recklessness. No, this was the work of an informant.

Who was the traitor? Konrad Leplow, a soldier in an anti-aircraft unit, lived at Hagenbeckallee 4 in Hamburg after the war, from at least 1969 to 1980.[3] In the 1970s, the Revolutionary Communist League (LCR) of France sent a request to its West German sister organization, the International Marxist Group (GIM). Rudolf Segall, now a leading member of the GIM, was asked to track down the Hamburg soldier. He forwarded the request to a GIM member in Hamburg whom we will call "Frank."[4] Frank could not find a public listing for Konrad Leplow, but since he worked for the city he was able to find an address via an official channel. "I thought up a story," Frank recalled more than 40 years later: "I went to the address with a product survey from [the market research company] Marplan. I would have filled out the questionnaire and then steered the conversation towards the times before '45. I would have asked if he had been in France."

Frank went to this address at least six times. The neighbors knew of a Leplow, but he was never at home. He was also said to have a holiday home in the Lüneburger Heath. Frank was able to find a second address there via the sales office of the holiday resort. "I went to the Lüneberg Heath three times with the questionnaire and camera equipment," he said, "but I never got the man in my view-finder." He sent a report to Segall – and never heard what was done with it.

A much younger member of one of the groups that emerged from the GIM, whom we will call "Max," heard of more ambitious plans. The idea was to kidnap the "traitor of the comrade Widelin" and hand him over to the French authorities. In the end, the plan was abandoned because they could not be sure of Leplow's identity.[5] No one knew whether Konrad had been an agent or perhaps just a comrade who capitulated under the pressure of the Gestapo.[6]

Konrad's betrayal had ripple effects that reached all the way to Paris. On October 6, 1943, Cruau was shot, as were a number of German soldiers. How many exactly? Craipeau spoke of 17. Thalmann said "roughly 15" were executed, while others were sent to the Eastern Front. Cobb wrote that 27 soldiers and sailors were arrested, ten of whom were shot.[7] It is impossible to find more precise information. The archives of the *Reichskriegsgericht* (Reich Court Martial) are arranged by the names of the accused, and since we do not know the same of a single soldier, these files cannot be found.[8]

The POI in Finistère, the department of Brest, was equally hit by the repression. The following day, the Gestapo arrested the POI's regional secretary, Marcel Beaufrère, its Kerhoun organizer, Yves Bodénez, the two Berthomé brothers, and further members. The Gestapo found addresses and was able to "roll up" the under-ground organization all the way to Paris. Three out of five members of the POI leadership – Roland Filiâtre, David Rousset, and Marcel Hic – were deported. In January of 1944, they were transferred to the Buchenwald concentration camp, and later to the neighboring subcamp Mittelbau-Dora. Hic, Bodénez, Georges Berthomé, and others never returned. Craipeau was one of the few leading Trotsky-ists who escaped the arrests and held the organization together until the end of the war. In total, up to 50 German soldiers and 50 French activists were arrested in early October of 1943.[9]

The soldiers' committees had been liquidated. The Trotskyist newspaper *La Verité* could now write about them for the first time – and tried to limit the damage:

> For two weeks the Gestapo has been working overtime. In an attempt to stop [...] our fraternization propaganda [...] it is hunting down our militants [...]. In its blindness the Gestapo is searching out and arresting without discrimination suspected Trotskyists, former activists, sympathetic trade unionists, and those who have abstained from any real activity since the beginning of the war. All those who have approached us, whether close or distant contacts, are being targeted. Everyone must be on their guard.[10]

Craipeau quoted this passage in his memoirs with the comment: "Of course, the article must not be taken at face value."[11] The Trotskyist editors were not just writing for sympathetic workers and young people, but also for the Gestapo and the Milice. They were trying to convince the secret police that they had arrested a number of innocent people, when in fact the authorities were relatively well informed about the Trotskyist organization, as Craipeau admitted. In order to strengthen the morale of readers in the face of these blows, two whole pages of *La Verité* were dedicated to successful experiences of fraternization. This is the source of the story about French workers and German soldiers in Brest greeting each other with raised fists.[12] It may be that "La Verité" invented this story in an attempt to convince the police that the internationalist movement in the Brest garrison was larger than the group that had been arrested. However, this was not the case – at least there was no further activity on the part of the soldiers' committees. Nor did Calvès think much of Craipeau's account of German soldiers displaying solidarity openly on the street: "Where does this absurd stuff come from?" he asked.[13]

Despite the repression, the Trotskyists were defiant:

> As for us: nothing will stop us, neither the inevitable provocations nor the arrests and torture they promise us. We know that

in extending a hand to the German worker in uniform we are attacking Hitlerism with greater effect than any terrorist assassinations could achieve. That the Gestapo has realized this – even if too late – is just more reason for us to continue.[14]

As many as 100 comrades had been arrested in a few days. Viktor, with his extensive experience underground, was able to escape – it is not clear how, but he fled back to Belgium. Just a month or two later, in November or December of 1943, he returned to Paris in the company of Ernest Mandel. This is where the first European conference of the Fourth International took place at the beginning of February of 1944. Viktor was a delegate of the German section (i.e. his small group of exiles) and continued to work in the international leadership.[15]

On May 1, 1944, *Arbeiter und Soldat* reappeared. Now it was no longer produced with a typewriter and a hectograph. Now it was a large printed newspaper – made in the same print shop as *La Verité*, which is why a number of German letters like ä, ö, ü, and ß are used only irregularly. This new version was no longer intended for discussion with small groups of sympathizers – it was an agitational broadsheet directed at the masses of German occupation soldiers "in the barracks, the clubs and the cinemas."[16] The rapid advance of the Allied armies was increasingly difficult to ignore. Wehrmacht soldiers wanted to know what to do.

Craipeau wrote that this relaunched newspaper was made by a commission consisting of "Widelin, Abosch (alias Béno), two German soldiers (Hans and Willie) and a cell of three French comrades."[17] Craipeau, while a leading figure of the French Trotskyists, was not directly involved in this work and his recollections were imprecise. Heinz Abosch (1918–97) was a young German refugee in France who had worked in the Trotskyists' International Youth Secretariat. However, by 1943 he was in Grenoble in the Italian occupation zone and had "broken with Trotsky and from all Marxist dogma."[18] One Trotskyist who certainly did collaborate on this German commission was Paul Hirzel (1918–69), whose family had fled from Silesia to Paris in 1933. After experiences in the Communist Youth and the social democratic scouts, the "Red Falcons," he joined the Revolutionary Socialist Youth that fused with the Trotskyists. During the occupation, Hirzel, a typographer, was responsible for the "technical apparatus" of the Internationalist Communist Party (PCI), which had been formed by the unification of different Trotskyist groups in May 1944. He was typesetting the new German broadsheet.[19]

Figure 10   "THE DECISION IS IN YOUR HANDS!" The headline of the June 1944 issue of *Worker and Soldier* called on German soldiers to organize for coming revolutionary struggles.

In June and July, two more issues of *Arbeiter und Soldat* were published. The entire July issue consisted of a long appeal to German soldiers – "The decision is in your hands!" – that sounds very much like Viktor (see Figure 10). He advised soldiers to organize themselves in revolutionary cells, hold on to their weapons, and establish links with local workers. He already saw the revolution on the horizon: "The day of the sailors and dockworkers of Kiel [from 1918] will return!" But Viktor did not live to see this day. By the time the August issue of *Arbeiter und Soldat* appeared, he had already been arrested and seriously injured.[20]

5.2. *"Never blame yourself"*: Arrest

On the morning of July 13, 1944, Christine Heymann went to a secret meeting place of the *résistance* in the Rue des Saints Pères in Paris.[21] Heymann had just turned 23 and was studying philosophy at the Sorbonne. Through a fellow student, she met Mathias Corvin from the POI and began working as a secretary for the Trotskyists.[22] She was going to the underground locale to request assistance for the POI's solidarity work. The Milice, however, had just raided the premises. They arrested Heymann as soon as she arrived and went to search her two apartments. The first one was near the Faubourg Poissonnière – this is where "Marcoux" lived, and he was arrested together with his partner. Marcoux was a pseudonym of Nicolas Spoulber, a Romanian POI member who worked in the European Secretariat of the Fourth International. Heymann's second apartment was a small room on the top floor of an apartment building on the Boulevard Saint-Michel in the Latin Quarter. Viktor lived in a different room just down the hall, but they only knew each other in passing.

"Unfortunately I had just paid the rent [for the second apartment] and still had the receipt," Heymann recalled in a letter in 1977.[23] The Milice thus found the address and searched her room, where they discovered a suitcase of German-language leaflets. Viktor "naturally assumed they had come for him." He attempted to escape over the roof, but was captured.

Heymann and Viktor were first taken to the headquarters of the Vichy regime's Anti-Communist Police Service (SPAC) on the Rue de Monceau. Spoulber and his partner were there too. Spoulber was locked up for the night in a room on the second floor and was able to jump out of a window.[24] Viktor was on the fourth floor and was trapped. After Spoulber's escape, the French police took out their anger on Viktor, beating him mercilessly: "We know who you are and what you are up to. If the other one had not fled, we would have let you go, but now we will hand you over to the Gestapo. They have wanted you for a long time."[25]

The following morning at 8 o'clock, the prisoners were picked up by Gestapo agents and transported to their headquarters on the Rue des Saussaies. Heymann, Janine (Spoulber's Romanian partner), and Viktor were all trapped in one room. "There was nothing but an oven that was full of ashes," Heymann wrote. "Widelin had hidden a razor blade and wanted to cut his wrists. Marcoux's partner prevented him from doing this and threw the blade into the ashes."[26]

The three prisoners faced a quite certain death. At this moment, Viktor told Heymann: "Never blame yourself for my arrest. This could have happened to me so many times already." Decades later she remembered his empathetic nature – even if she could not remember much else. Due to the traumatic events, her memories were jumbled, as she admitted.

There is a slightly different chronology in an obituary for "Marcel Widelin" in *La Verité* in 1946. According to this text, Heymann and Viktor were "mercilessly tortured by a whole gang of executioners" at SPAC headquarters for eight days before being handed over to the Gestapo on July 21. We cannot know for sure.[27] In any case, at some point Heymann was taken to the military prison in Fresnes. Here the Gestapo continued to interrogate her. She never saw Viktor again – yet also never forgot him. Heymann was deported to the transit camp Romainville and from there to the concentration camp Ravensbrück. She survived the war.

The Gestapo tortured Viktor. They asked him: "Well, boy, who do you think is going to win the war?" Viktor could not resist panache: "Definitely not Hitler." They asked if he was a Jew. He replied: "I am proud of it." Viktor had given up his Zionism, but not his identity. He was later able to report to a comrade: "They began to beat me and broke one of my ribs. The interrogation lasted for days, but they learned nothing from me. After a few days – I don't know exactly how many since I lost track of time in the basement – they took me away."[28]

Two German soldiers and two officers put Viktor in handcuffs. They got into a car and told him they were going to the military prison in Fresnes where he would be tried by a German court. The road from the Gestapo office on the north bank of the Seine to the prison went 17 kilometers due south into a suburb. But the German car did not drive south. They went east into the Bois de Vincennes, the largest park in Paris, where the *Parc Zoologique* had opened its doors ten years earlier.

5.3. *"The Gestapo shot me dead": Two Executions*

"The Gestapo shot me dead." Viktor was lying in a bed in the Rothschild Hospital in Paris. It was a Jewish hospital under German administration – all the staff were forced to wear yellow stars. Viktor's head and chest were wrapped in bandages. His face was "pale and sunken." Paul Thalmann had just entered the room. Viktor smiled faintly and whispered to his former housemate. He had been lying there for eight days. It was the afternoon of August 1, 1944, and Thalmann had just received a telephone call from a nurse. Victor began to explain what had happened.[29]

Driving through the Bois de Vincennes, the Gestapo car had turned onto a small road. Viktor knew the Germans intended to shoot him "while attempting to escape." This was a well-established method for German police to dispose of revolutionaries – Karl Liebknecht had met the same fate 25 years prior. The car stopped and Viktor was told to get out. "Without saying a word, one of the officers put a gun to his head and pulled the trigger." He fell to the floor, seriously injured, and was shot again in the chest. Yet he was not dead. At some point a stranger on a bicycle approached and grabbed Viktor's shoulders. "Gestapo, Gestapo," he whispered, before passing out. The stranger was a French policeman. He called a police car that took Viktor to the Rothschild Hospital, where he was operated upon. "One bullet was stuck in his head, and another had grazed his heart." After a week in a coma, on July 31, he regained consciousness.

"So, here I am, executed by the Gestapo," Viktor chuckled. And so much had happened during the weeks of torture and unconsciousness! On July 20, Nazi generals had attempted to assassinate Hitler – even in the highest circles of the fascist regime, the impending defeat was beyond doubt. Allied troops advanced relentlessly toward the French capital. Thalmann recalled how Viktor took the news: "His eyes glistened and he smiled again. 'I hope I live to see that day'."

Viktor gave two secret addresses of the Trotskyist organization to Thalmann, who immediately took off on his bicycle. At the first address, he met the wife of Michel Raptis (known by his pseudonym Pablo) from the European Secretariat. She said: "Why did you come here? I don't know you, or a Viktor, I have nothing to do with any of this." After ten minutes of discussion, Thalmann was able to gain her trust and she admitted the organization was already aware of Viktor's fate. He could not stay in the hospital for long – it was too dangerous. "By the way, we have a comrade who is a doctor in the hospital looking after Viktor," she said.

The following day, August 2, Thalmann returned to the hospital. Viktor reported that a doctor had examined him in the morning. An unknown man stood behind the doctor holding up a metro ticket with Viktor's real name written on the back. Viktor answered the silent question with a nod – but did not know who the man was. Viktor assumed this was a comrade sent to check on him, but understood that he needed to escape. "If I stay here too long, they will come for me again," he said. He told Thalmann that he had no confidence in the Trotskyist organization – Thalmann's group needed to break him out of the hospital.[30]

Viktor had been in the hospital for nine days. At any moment the Gestapo would learn of his survival – either from the police officer who discovered him in the park or from the hospital administration. Thalmann's group held a "council of war" at their house. They had a submachine gun and two revolvers buried in the garden. But they lacked a car to transport the patient. The Jewish staff at the Rothschild Hospital would certainly allow Viktor to leave – but it had to look as if they had been coerced.

By the end of the day, the plan was complete: Three comrades would call an ambulance, and when it arrived they would threaten the drivers with guns, forcing them to drive to the Rothschild Hospital. Two of the hijackers would then enter the hospital, brandishing weapons, and get Viktor out, while the third stood guard outside. They would put Viktor in the ambulance and have it drive past Versailles to the Vallée de Chevreuse. There they would send the ambulance drivers off and "threaten them with the vengeance of the *résistance* if they reported what had happened." Then they would use a wheelbarrow to transport Viktor to a safe house in the countryside.

On August 3, Pierre, one of Thalmann's comrades, went to the hospital to inform Viktor of the plan. He returned to the house an hour later. Viktor was gone! Less than a quarter of an hour after Thalmann's visit the day before, the Gestapo had come for Viktor. Nobody knew where they had taken him.

After a few days, rumors seeped through that Viktor was being held in the German military hospital on the Boulevard de l'Hôpital. Visitors were not allowed. A woman from Thalmann's group managed to speak to the hospital's Protestant military chaplain. He assured her that even he did not have access to the ward for terrorists. The hospital's director eventually confirmed that a man matching Viktor's description had been admitted to that ward. For three days – it must have been August 5–8 – Thalmann and his comrades kept watch in front of the military hospital.

Allied troops were now on the outskirts of the city. Would they arrive in time? The Germans were evacuating. Around the clock, trucks and ambulances were transporting people and equipment out of the hospital. Was Viktor in one of these vehicles, alive or dead? We do not know.

Viktor's exact fate is unknown. Similar to the character Jill Layton in Terry Gilliam's film "Brazil," one could say that he was murdered twice.[31] Martin Monath alias Monte alias Paul Widelin alias Viktor died at 31. During the war he had escaped the Nazis time and again, but in the final days his luck ran out. On August 15, about a week after the evacuation of the hospital, the *résistance* called a general strike in Paris. The Nazis' murder apparatus remained in motion until the last moment: That night, a final deportation train left Paris for Buchenwald and Ravensbrück. On August 19, the French resistance fighters began an insurrection. On August 25, the remaining German troops surrendered. Viktor did not live to see that day.

According to Prager, Viktor was killed in a Gestapo "lair."[32] According to historian Philippe Bourrinet, he was probably dragged off by the fleeing Germans and hung with a rope.[33] Though it is tempting to search for closure to this story, the Nazis left no records of how Viktor's life ended. All we can say for sure is that 22 years later, on July 3, 1967, a West Berlin court declared that "Martin Ludwig Witlin" was dead. His date of death was set as May 8, 1945.[34] One year later, his siblings received reparations totaling 10,000 Deutschmarks – roughly one year's average salary in West Germany at the time.[35]

5.4. "Illusions about Council Germany": Is Thalmann a Reliable Witness?

Thalmann provided the most comprehensive recollections of Viktor's time in Paris. But how reliable is his account? Thalmann described how Viktor came to agree with him politically. Viktor might have formally remained a member of the Fourth International, but he collaborated mostly with Thalmann and in his heart shared the latter's criticisms of Trotskyism:

> Viktor was [...] no longer the intransigent Trotskyist of days past; the dealings with us, the heated discussions, the links to other revolutionary groups, the particularly obstinate attitude of the French Trotskyists, coupled with their organizational incompetence, had modified his original views significantly. Nonetheless, he stuck with his organization.[36]

Thalmann provided no evidence for his claims – and his own recollections are contradictory.

In the two letters Thalmann sent to Jakob Moneta in 1970, while writing his memoirs, he only recalled the newspaper *Arbeiter und Soldat* vaguely. First he described a publication in German and French – in a postscript he corrected himself, after his wife had reminded him that *Arbeiter und Soldat* was only in German. He claimed: "Viktor and I took turns writing the lead articles."[37] But then he added that he def-

initely did not have anything to do with "the issue from June [1944],"
since "we did not really have these illusions about council Germany,
quite the contrary."[38] However, the slogan of a "council Germany"
(with a government based on workers' and soldiers' councils) appears
in almost every issue of the newspaper. The second issue (August
1943) contains a whole article on the topic. This "illusion" was the
programmatic basis of the entire project. If Thalmann had nothing
to do with this, what exactly was he involved with? In his autobiography he recalled "about four issues," likely referring to the three
issues from 1943. He did not appear to have been aware of the three
issues from 1944 – no longer produced in Thalmann's house, but in
the print shop of the French Trotskyists – until he received facsimiles
from Jakob Moneta in 1970.

Did the editor of *Arbeiter und Soldat* move away from the Fourth
International? The first issue presents itself as an "organ for proletarian revolutionary unification," which would correspond to the
interfactional project described by Thalmann. The second and third
issues, however, added "Fourth International" to the subtitle. In 1944,
the newspaper appeared as the "Organ of the League of Communist-
Internationalists (German section of the Fourth International)" – and
even if such a section barely existed, the political orientation could
not have been clearer. In the first issues, there was no theoretical discussion of the Russian question. The second issue even contained the
ambiguous statement that Stalin's regime had "nothing in common
with socialism" – a formulation that could encompass both analyses.
The fifth issue, however, contained an article describing Russia as
"a degenerate workers' state, governed by a parasite bureaucracy." In
line with Trotsky's position, the newspaper called for a defense of the
USSR and a struggle against the Stalinist regime. Nothing we know
about Viktor suggests that he would have written and published
Trotskyist positions that he did not believe in, purely out of loyalty
to his organization.

In his autobiography, Thalmann claimed *Arbeiter und Soldat* for
himself. "We were the only ones who succeeded in forming soldiers'
cells in Hitler's army" (at least in France).[39] His "we" refers to himself
and Viktor, but explicitly excludes the Trotskyists outside of Brest.
Thalmann may well have distributed the newspaper in Paris: "We

put it in mailboxes, in doorways, on windowsills of German soldiers' hostels, and in German trucks."[40] Yet he did not mention ever having contact with German soldiers himself. Nor did Thalmann mention the French Trotskyists who actually built these cells – and who sacrificed their lives to do so – like Robert Cruau.

His account of Viktor's death is contradictory as well. "The [French] Trotskyists did absolutely nothing," Thalmann wrote.[41] Yet he reported himself that the Trotskyist organization had a doctor in the hospital looking after Viktor. Thalmann visited Viktor on August 1 – on August 2, Yvan Craipeau from the Trotskyist organization was also there.[42]

Thalmann provides important information – yet it seems he was eager to exaggerate his own role while downplaying the work of his Trotskyist ex-comrades. There is no evidence that Viktor moved away from Trotskyism. Thalmann likely collaborated on the first three issues of *Arbeiter und Soldat* in 1943, but had nothing to do with the three issues in 1944. We can assume that Viktor remained a staunch Trotskyist and leading member of the Fourth International until his death.

The Revolutionary Communists of Germany (RKD), who had also broken with Trotskyism during the war, also claimed Viktor as a sympathizer. In a report from 1947 they wrote:

> Comrade Widelin, coming from the socialist-zionist camp, was won for revolutionary Marxist ideas in Belgium by our comrade Duhl. He worked in the Belgian Trotskyist movement during the war, but was under our influence from the beginning. When he published the first issues of *Arbeiter und Soldat* in 1943, there was close collaboration between him and our existing movement. Comrade Widelin rejected the "defensist" and bureaucratic positions of the I.S. [the International Secretariat of the Fourth International].[43]

Further, the report claims that Viktor was "arrested and shot by the Gestapo due to the criminal negligence of the I.S." This is, as we have seen, a slander. It was the inexperience of a young sympathizer, combined with terrible luck, that led to Viktor's arrest. Furthermore, the International Secretariat of the Fourth International, which had moved to New York in 1940, had absolutely no influence on events in occupied France. A European Secretariat was based in Paris – and Viktor himself was a member. It would appear that Thalmann's left communists and the Trotskyists spent the following years and decades accusing each other of having put the Gestapo on Viktor's trail. However, there is no evidence to assign blame to one side or the other. More likely is that the information about the whereabouts of the seriously injured revolutionary reached the German police via normal bureaucratic channels. The Gestapo would have been zealously searching for this Jewish communist anyway.

6

Conclusion

What did Viktor accomplish in his short life (see Figure 11)? If we look for a pragmatic answer to the question, the only honest answer is: Not much. Or maybe: He left behind some shreds of paper and a few dead soldiers.

The Italian communist Antonio Gramsci argued in his prison notebooks that the work of a revolutionary leadership can be judged by two criteria: "1. in what it actually does; 2. in what provision it makes for the eventuality of its own destruction. It is difficult to say which of these two facts is the more important. Since defeat in the struggle must always be envisaged, the preparation of one's own successors is as important as what one does for victory."[1] In this second, perhaps more important sense, we should ask what Viktor left behind for the revolutionary movement.

The bourgeoisie does not normally rule with sheer force, but instead relies on the hegemony of its ideas. Its subjects are simply incapable of imagining social relations other than those of bourgeois society. The 31 years Martin Monath spent on this earth were a single cry against the supposedly unchangeable nature of things. Society was infested with antisemitism? Then he would build a new society in Palestine! And when that plan reached its limits, Martin's ambitions only grew: Then he would have to root out all forms of exploitation and oppression via world revolution!

Viktor's story is not just a story of personal courage. Countless people displayed courage in the fight against fascism. Viktor, however, had the ability to develop his resistance outside of the limits of bourgeois hegemony. In a uniquely reactionary situation, he was able to use the tools of Marxism to show how the Nazis' murder apparatus could be smashed, by exploiting the class contradictions within the Wehrmacht. This understanding strengthened his courage. As his

Figure 11 Martin Monath as a teenager.
Photographer unknown, from the private
archive of Naomi Baitner.

teacher Leon Trotsky wrote: "Marxism is, in its very essence, a set of
directives for revolutionary action. Marxism does not overlook will
and courage, but rather aids them to find the right road."[2]

Ernest Mandel wrote these lines about Abraham Leon, which
could just as easily apply to Viktor:

The situation seemed to justify only resignation and watchful
waiting. Any other attitude appeared like a manifestation of
desperate and impotent revolt. What was lacking was not so much
courage to act as courage to think, and to think correctly. Marxist
analysis enabled one to penetrate through the totalitarian lid
pressing on Europe and to discover there gestating forces which
would in the end throw it off. Correctly establishing the reasons
which we had for hope, Leon noted that the workers' movement
in Europe had already reached the lowest point of its ebb. It was
now necessary to count upon a new rise. It was necessary not to

await it passively but to prepare for it, preparing for it the cadres and insofar as possible the masses. [...] Behind every reason for despair, one must discover a reason for hope.[3]

At the beginning of the Second World War, the bourgeoisie told many – often contradictory – stories about how the world worked: Stories about thousand-year empires of master races, stories about capitalist democracy as the ideal form of human society, stories about great clashes between nations that could only end with the complete defeat of one or the other; above all, the bourgeoisie told of a great struggle between fascism and democracy – as if the barbarism of the Nazis could only be beaten by supporting "democratic" colonial empires. With hardly more than a typewriter, Viktor repudiated all these stories. He showed that the inconceivable slaughter between armies of millions was ultimately a struggle between the possessors and the dispossessed – and it could be ended by the latter's victory.

The bourgeoisie further claimed (and continues to claim) that antisemitism is something eternal that can only be held back by sepa-rating Jews from all other societies in their own nation-state. Viktor, an organizer of the Zionist movement for many years, also rejected this bourgeois myth. He aimed to solve the Jewish question by over-throwing capitalism. Again we can ask pragmatically: Did history prove the Zionists right? Could Viktor have survived – like much of his family – if he had fled to Palestine? Could continued work for the *aliyah* have saved more Jewish lives? There are two answers to this.

From a military perspective, we can say that Palestine was by no means a safe haven for Europe's Jews. The problem was not just the strict limitations on immigration imposed by the British mandate. In 1942, the German Afrika Korps was advancing rapidly toward the Middle East. An *Einsatzgruppe Ägypten* (Task Force Egypt) of the SS was preparing to annihilate the Jewish population of Palestine.[4] The Zionist militia Hagana was debating plans for its final stand – there was talk of a "Masada" at Mount Carmel, i.e. a biblical and hopeless final battle of the Jews against the Nazis.[5] Only the British victory in the second battle of El Alamein in early November 1942 prevented a genocide. The Jewish colony in Palestine could have easily been turned into a huge death camp.

But the moral element is far more important. Viktor *did not want to escape*. Again and again he rejected opportunities to flee. He chose to continue the revolutionary struggle against Nazi rule in Europe. It went against Viktor's whole character to bow down to Hitler's temporary power. Even when he had to escape from Paris to Brussels after so many of his comrades were killed by the Gestapo, he returned to the lion's den as quickly as possible to resume his work.

In Gramsci's terms we can say that Viktor achieved nothing – and also created an example for future generations that survived long after his own destruction. In the face of capitalism's greatest slaughter (until now), Viktor presented an alternative to chauvinism. Had there been 1,000 or 10,000 Viktors in France – or more precisely: had there been 1,000 or 10,000 Bolshevik cadres – the whole world war might have turned out differently. Like Karl Liebknecht, Viktor kept the flame of proletarian internationalism alive during the darkest hours. It is these periods of black reaction that bring forth the most brilliant revolutionaries. As Russian poet Apollon Maykov once wrote: "The darker the night, the brighter the stars."

Notes

Chapter 1

1. 'Proletaires de tous les pays, unissez-vous! Proleten aller Laender, vereinigt euch!' in *La Verité* (Paris), October 15, 1943, reprinted in Jean-Michel Brabant, ed., *Fac-simile de 'La Vérité' clandestine: 1940-1944* (Paris: ÉDI, 1978), 139. Did this scene really take place as described? We will investigate that in Section 5.1.
2. Ibid. (our translation).
3. André Calvès talks about 27 soldiers in the organization. André Calvès, "La trahison de Conrad Leplow Octobre 1943," manuscript in the BDIC in Paris, probably from 1944, http://andre-calves.org/autres%20redactions/La%20trahison%20de%20Conrad%20LEPLOW%20octobre%201943.htm. Yvan Craipeau speaks of 50 soldiers. Yvan Craipeau, *Swimming Against the Tide: Trotskyists in German Occupied France* (London: Merlin Press, 2012), 245.
4. André Calvès, *Sans bottes ni médailles: Un trotskyste breton dans la guerre* (Montreuil: Editions La Brèche, 1984), 75 (our translation).
5. Craipeau, *Swimming*, 245.
6. Christine Botzet (Federal Archive of Germany, Military Archive Department), e-mail message to author, November 29, 2016.
7. Clara and Paul Thalmann, *Revolution für die Freiheit: Stationen eines politischen Kampfes Moskau / Madrid / Paris* (Hamburg: Verlag Association, 1977), 316 (our translation).
8. Paul Ehrlich, Letter to Jakob Moneta, July 5, 1970, Rodolphe Prager papers, folder 301, IISG, Amsterdam (our translation).
9. Martin Monath, Letter to Karl Monath, undated, Rodolphe Prager papers, folder 301, IISG, Amsterdam (our translation). (Henceforth all letters from Martin Monath to his siblings will be numbered and quoted in the format "Monte, Letter 1." All these letters are available in German at www.klassegegenklasse.org/arbeiterundsoldat/.)
10. Thalmann, *Revolution*, 338 (our translation).
11. Ehrlich, Letter (our translation).
12. Wolfgang Abendroth, *Einführung in die Geschichte der Arbeiterbewegung: Band I* (Heilbronn: Distel, 1985), 187 (our translation). Three decades later, the young historian Ralf Hoffrogge was able to show that Müller, after ending his work in the KPD and later as a historian, became a realty

speculator before dying in 1943. Ralf Hoffrogge, *Working-Class Politics in the German Revolution: Richard Müller, the Revolutionary Shop Stewards and the Origins of the Council Movement* (Leiden: Brill, 2014).

13. Rodolphe Prager, Interview with Ernest Mandel, November 12, 1977, Rodolphe Prager papers, folder 290, IISG, Amsterdam, quoted in Jan Willem Stutje, *Ernest Mandel: A Rebel's Dream Deferred* (London: Verso, 2009), 25 (Stutje's translation).

14. Thalmann, *Revolution*, 343 (our translation).

15. Stutje, *Mandel*, 25.

16. Marguerite Baget, "A Heroic Trotskyist Leader in the German Underground," and George Breitman, "Why The Gestapo Tracked Him Down," *The Militant* (New York), July 20, 1946. The *Cahiers Leon Trotsky*, the historical magazine edited by Pierre Broué, also referred to him this way in the 1990s. "Michael Pablo," *Cahiers Leon Trotsky*, 57 (March 1996), 120.

17. Marguerite Baget, "Nous accusons les bourreaux de la S.P.A.C. d'avoir assassiné Marcel Widelin," *La Verité* (Paris), January 6, 1946.

18. Wolfgang Alles, "Cyrano von Bergerac und die Geduld des Revolutionärs" (Interview with Rudolf Segall), *Inprekorr* (Cologne), 414/15 and 416/417 (May/June and July/August 2006).

19. Robert J. Alexander, *International Trotskyism* (Durham, NC: Duke University Press, 1991), 426. Matthew Cobb, *The Resistance: The French Fight Against the Nazis* (London: Simon & Schuster, 2009) 210.

20. "File: Stolperstein Muskauer Str 24 (Kreuz) Martin Monath.jpg," https://commons.wikimedia.org/wiki/File:Stolperstein_Muskauer_Str_24_(Kreuz)_Martin_Monath.jpg.

21. Neither in the local Registry Offices *[Standesämter]* nor in the central residents' register *[Einwohnermeldekartei]*. Correspondence with these archives, September 2016.

22. Reg. Nr. 700 532 (Martin Ludwig Monath-Wittlin), Berlin Reparations Office *[Entschädigungsbehörde]*.

Chapter 2

1. Bertolt Brecht, "In Praise of Dialectics," quoted in Ernst Fisher, *The Necessity of Art: A Marxist Approach* (Middlesex: Penguin Books, 1963), 115.

2. Paul Frölich, *Im radikalen Lager: Politische Autobiographie 1890–1921* (Berlin: Basisdruck, 2013), 311 (our translation).

3. Ibid.

4. Baruch and Emilie Monath is the spelling used by their daughter Lotte Teppich in an entry in Yad Vashem in 1985 (available online at yvng.yadvashem.org). Naomi Baitner, interview with the author, August 29, 2016. Naomi Baitner is the daughter of Lotte Teppich (née Monath) and

the niece of Martin Monath. Karl Monath, applying for reparations in 1955, wrote that his father had moved from Vienna to Berlin in 1902. This might have been an attempt to make the family appear more "German" to the miserly authorities in West Berlin. Reg. Nr. 274 068 (Karol Wittlin), Berlin Reparations Office *[Entschädigungsbehörde]*.

5. Reg. Nr. 700 532.

6. Akte zur Auswanderung von Hans und Lotte Teppich im Jahr 1933, Akte A4257, Bestand Rep. 36A, Oberfinanzpräsident Berlin-Brandenburg, Main Archive of the *Land* Brandenburg, Potsdam.

7. There is even uncertainty about Martin's exact birthday. On the commemorative stone in Kreuzberg, as well as in two entries at Yad Vashem, his birth year is listed as 1912. (Besides the entry quoted above, there is a second one for "Martin Monat-Wittlin," placed there in 1990 by his niece Naomi Baitner.) But in his asylum application in Belgium in 1939, he entered 1913 as his year of birth. File A.353.075, Justice Ministry, Foreigners' Police, State Archives of Belgium, Brussels. The birthday of Karl Monath can be found in a certificate from the Jewish Community of Berlin from the year 1958, private archive of Naomi Baitner.

8. Ehrlich, Letter.

9. Antrag Bernhard Monath, Gesellschaft mit beschränkter Haftung, Vertrieb von Herrengarderobe. Bestand A Rep 342-02, Nr. 13656, Amtsgericht Berlin, Archive of the *Land* Berlin (our translation). Thanks to Heidi Sow for this reference.

10. The explanation: When the Gestapo executed Monath in early August 1944 – just a few weeks before fleeing Paris – they did not produce a death certificate. Therefore it cannot be excluded that Monath is still alive somewhere – hidden from his relatives and comrades for 70 years, and now almost 105! Who knows? 110 years after his birth, in the year 2023, the birth certificate will be released. Correspondence with the Registry Office of Treptow-Köpenick between September and November of 2016. Even a court document from 1967 certifying Monath's death was not enough to convince them. Additional correspondence, February 2019. However, the files from the Reparations Office make numerous references to the information on the birth certificate.

11. Reg. Nr. 274 068.

12. Antrag Bernhard Monath.

13. Baitner, Interview (our translation).

14. Ehrlich, Letter (our translation).

15. Reg. Nr. 700 532.

16. She read this letter to her own daughter, decades later and on a different continent. Baitner, Interview (our translation).

17. Ehrlich, Letter (our translation).

18. To be precise: From 1904 to 1911, the store was in the Skalitzer Straße 122. In 1912, it was one door down, in the Skalitzer Straße 123, but in 1913 it was back at number 122. In 1914, there was no listing, but in 1915 the shop reappeared in the 122–3. From 1918 onwards, the Monath GmbH was only in the Skalitzer Straße 123, and stayed at this address until 1930. Berlin Address Directories from 1900 to 1940, Archive of the *Land* Berlin.

19. Now the Bulgarische Straße, behind the Treptower Park. See the city plan of Berlin from 1907, www.blocksignal.de/krt/f.php?k=blo7&r=4&i=1932.

20. Antrag Bernhard Monath (our translation). Karl Monath, applying for reparations in 1955, provided several affidavits claiming that his father had a "flourishing" business and planned to finance both his sons' university studies, making no mention of his bankruptcy or his death. This appears to be an – absolutely legitimate – attempt to sway the authorities, who paid reparations based on material loss. Reg. Nr. 274 068.

21. Bundesarchiv, *Gedenkbuch*, www.bundesarchiv.de/gedenkbuch/de1181248.

22. Ehrlich, Letter (our translation).

23. Ibid.

24. Karl Monath, Letter to Lotte Teppich, undated, probably 1937 or 1938, private archive of Naomi Baitner (our translation). (Letter 1.)

25. Reg. Nr. 700 532. "Geschichte der Nürtingen-Grundschule," www. nuertingen-grundschule.de/schulweb/geschichte-der-schule.html.

26. Baitner, Interview (our translation).

27. Ehrlich, Letter (our translation).

28. The archives of the Berlin Senate Administration for Education, Youth and Science only go back to 1947. Older records were probably destroyed. Gerit Geßner, e-mail message to the author, September 20, 2016.

29. Reg. Nr. 700 532.

30. Carina Baganz, *Diskriminierung, Ausgrenzung, Vertreibung: Die Technische Hochschule Berlin während des Nationalsozialismus* (Berlin: Metropol, 2013).

31. "Unfortunately there is a gap in the student enrollment records from 1930–1935. […] As far as we know, this gap is due to the fact that enrollment at this time was to be shifted to a new card system. And the records of this new system in all likelihood fell victim to the effects of the war." Dagmar Spies (Archive of the Technical University Berlin), e-mail message to the author, September 21, 2016 (our translation). In the same year, Leon Sedov, the oldest son of Leon Trotsky, studied engineering at the Technical University. Pierre Broué, "In Germany for the International," *Revolutionary History*, 9/4 (2008), 237–61.

32. Ernst Piper, "Als der 1. Mai braun wurde," *Spiegel Online*, Einestages, April 30, 2008 (our translation).

33. Alles, "Cyrano." Rudolf Segall, "'Die Gestapo hat mich erschossen': Leben und Tod eines deutsch-jüdischen Widerstandskämpfers', *Bresche* (Zurich), 89/11 (1989), 31–4.

34. Baget, "Heroic Trotskyist."

35. Ehrlich, Letter (our translation).

36. Suska Döpp, *Jüdische Jugendbewegung in Köln 1906-1938* (Münster: LIT Verlag, 1997), 64–7 (our translation).

37. Rafael Medoff, *Historical Dictionary of Zionism,* (New York: Routledge, 2012), 80–1.

38. Ibid., 77–8.

39. Joel Beinin, *Was the Red Flag Flying There? Marxist Politics and the Arab-Israeli Conflict in Egypt and Israel, 1948–1965* (Berkeley: University of California Press, 1990), 26–30. Beinin argues that Hashomer Hatzair experienced continuous "tension between its commitment to revolutionary-socialist internationalism on the one hand and Zionism on the other." In each crisis, however, the majority of the group gave priority to their Zionist commitments.

40. Eli Ashkenazi, "Hashomer Hatzair Youth Movement Comes Full Circle With Relaunch in Germany," *Ha'aretz* (Tel Aviv), October 9, 2011.

41. Ehrlich, Letter.

42. Karl Monath, Letter 1 (our translation).

43. Daniel Kahn and Oy Division, "Oy Ir Narishe Tsienistn/Oh You Foolish Little Zionists/Глупые Сионисты," www.haggadot.com/clip/lyrics-oy-ir-narishe-tsienistn-oh-you-foolish-little-zionists-глупые-сионисты. Fiedler formulates it as follows: The Zionist attempt at a "'modern solution to the Jewish question' (Theodor Herzl) stood in opposition to an emancipatory hope in a kind of 'red assimilation', which promised to secure the emancipation and integration of the Jews into their non-Jewish environment in a communist future." Lutz Fiedler, *Matzpen: Eine andere israelische Geschichte* (Göttingen: Vandenhoeck & Ruprecht, 2017), 307 (our translation).

44. See for example the experiences of Werner Scholem, a leading member of the left wing of the KPD, with antisemitic attacks in the mid-1920s. Ralf Hoffrogge, *A Jewish Communist in Weimar Germany: The Life of Werner Scholem (1895–1940)* (Leiden: Brill, 2017), 302–4, especially footnote 24. For a more general discussion of antisemitism in the KPD see: Ralf Hoffrogge, "Der Sommer des Nationalbolschewismus? Die Stellung der KPD-Linken zum Ruhrkampf und ihre Kritik am "Schlageter-Kurs' von 1923," *Sozial.Geschichte Online* (Duisburg-Essen), 20 (2017), 99–146; Gerhard Hanloser, "Die Rote Fahne und der Antisemitismus: Olaf Kisten-machers Präsentation tatsächlicher und vermeintlicher antijüdischer Aussagen in der KPD-Tageszeitung," Ibid., 175–96. In this question, Hoffrogge has it right: There was antisemitism in the rank and file of the

workers' parties, but significantly less than in other parties. Only during the process of Stalinization did antisemitism blossom in the KPD.

45. Ernest Mandel [Germain], "A. Leon," *Fourth International* (New York), 8/6 (June 1947), 172–6.

46. Alles, "Cyrano" (our translation).

47. Alfred Rosenberg, *Die Spur des Juden im Wandel der Zeit* (Munich: Zentralverlag der NSDAP, 1937), 153 (our translation).

48. Ibid., 151 (our translation).

49. Winston Churchill, "Zionism versus Bolshevism," *Illustrated Sunday Herald* (London), February 8, 1920.

50. Quoted in Ashkenazi, "Hashomer."

51. Leon Trotsky, "Chances in Germany," *Hashomer Hatzair* (Warsaw), 13 (October 1933). "When Does the End Come?" *Hashomer Hatzair* (Warsaw), 14 (November 1933). Thanks to Yossi Bartal for this reference. The article was originally published as: "Deutsche Perspektiven," *Neue Weltbühne* (Prague), July 27 and August 3, 1933. An English translation was published as "German Perspectives", *Class Struggle* (New York), 3/9 and 3/10 (October 1933 and November 1933).

52. Quoted in Trotsky, "German Perspectives."

53. Ibid.

54. Alles, "Cyrano" (our translation).

55. There is an indirect mention of Trotsky in the issue of February 1934: Sasha Korin reported on a meeting of the London Bureau in which representatives of the (Trotskyist) International Communist League participated. The author rejected their proposal for the foundation of a Fourth International. Sasha Korin, "In the International Workers' Movement," *Hashomer Hatzair* (Warsaw), 1–4 (February 1934).

56. Peter Berens, *Trotzkisten gegen Hitler* (Cologne: Neuer ISP Verlag, 2007), 60. Alexander, *Trotskyism*, 419.

57. Alles, "Cyrano" (our translation).

58. The German Trotskyist leader Anton Grylewicz reported in mid-1932 that his organization had published "roughly 67,000 copies of the different pamphlets of comrade Trotsky" in the previous year. Anton Grylewicz, "Die Entwicklung der deutschen Opposition," in Annegret Schüle, *Trotzkismus in Deutschland bis 1933: "Für die Arbeitereinheitsfront zur Abwehr des Faschismus'* (Cologne: Self-published, 1989), 133–5 (our translation); Fritz Hermann, "Jakob Moneta: Interview zum achtzigsten Geburtstag," *Inprekorr* (Cologne), 278 (December 1994).

59. Ehrlich, Letter (our translation).

60. Hermann, "Moneta" (our translation).

61. Susanne Urban, ed., *"Rettet die Kinder!" Die Jugend-Aliyah 1933 bis 2003: Einwanderung und Jugendarbeit in Israel* (Frankfurt/Main: Kinder- und Jugend-Aliyah Deutschland, 2003), 36.

62. Karl Monath, Letter to Lotte Teppich, undated, probably 1934, private archive of Naomi Baitner (our translation). (Letter 2.)

63. Monte, "Ein Brief von der Hachschara," August 1934, Faxe (Denmark), source unknown, probably a yearbook of Hashomer Hatzair, Rodolphe Prager papers, folder 301, IISG, Amsterdam (our translation). All further quotes in this section, unless otherwise marked, are from this document.

64. "R." refers to Rudolf Segall, as Ehrlich reported.

65. Alles, "Cyrano" (our translation).

66. Ibid. (our translation).

67. Segall, "Gestapo" (our translation).

68. Ehrlich, Letter. We know even less about Lola Aftergut than we do about Monte. According to an entry in Yad Vashem, she was born in Poland in 1917 (making her four years younger than Monte) and spent the war years in Berlin. According to another entry, she was born in Berlin in 1921 (making her eight years younger than Monte) and lived in Warsaw during the war. Both entries agree with Ehrlich's account that she was murdered in the Warsaw Ghetto. It is unlikely that these entries are for different people, since the parents' names are each listed as Max and Rosa Aftergut (available online at yvng.yadvashem.org).

69. A coup de main is a sudden military attack based on speed and surprise. This seems like the best translation for the original term *Husarenstückchen* (German: small hussar piece) for a daring and successful endeavor. It refers to the hussars, the central European light cavalry of the late seventeenth and eighteenth century renowned for their bold military operations.

70. Ehrlich, Letter (our translation). Monte's Polish citizenship is confirmed in his asylum application in Belgium in 1939.

71. Segall, "Gestapo."

72. "Nachtrag zum Geburts-Neben [*sic*]," Registry Office Berlin-Treptow, February 13, 1939, private archive of Naomi Baiter (our translation).

73. For an explanation of why we can't see his birth certificate, see Section 2.1.

74. Segall, "Gestapo."

75. Alles, "Cyrano."

76. Ibid. (our translation).

77. Ibid. (our translation).

78. "Jakob Moneta wird 85," *Avanti* (Cologne), 44 (November 1999), (our translation).

79. Alles, "Cyrano." For the name of the group see "Jakob Moneta wird 85." For the development of the Trotskyist group in Palestine in the 1930s, see Fiedler, *Matzpen*, 90–8.

80. This is a reference to the phrase "actually existing socialism," or "actually existing socialism," a popular term for the Eastern Bloc.

81. Alina Bothe and Gertrud Pickhan, eds., *Ausgewiesen! Berlin, 28.10.1938: Die Geschichte der "Polenaktion"* (Berlin: Metropol, 2018).

82. Raphael Gross, *November 1938: Die Katastrophe vor der Katastrophe* (Munich: C.H. Beck, 2013), 19 (our translation).

83. Quoted in "Stalinists Try to 'Smear' Grynszpan," *Socialist Appeal* (New York), December 17, 1938.

84. Ibid. The title page of this issue of the paper was dedicated to the SWP's campaign to admit Jewish refugees from Europe into the United States. The headline cries in capital letters: "Let us in or we will perish!" A box demands: "Open the Doors to Europe's Refugees!"

85. Leon Trotsky, "For Grynszpan: Against Fascist Pogrom Gangs and Stalinist Scoundrels," *Socialist Appeal* (New York), February 14, 1939.

86. Leon Trotsky, "Why Marxists Oppose Individual Terrorism," originally published in German in *Der Kampf* (Vienna), November 1911, English translation from the Marxists Internet Archive, www.marxists.org/archive/trotsky/1911/11/tia09.htm.

87. Trotsky, "For Grynszpan."

88. Reg. Nr. 274 068.

89. Segall, "Gestapo" (our translation).

Chapter 3

1. Monte, Letter 3 (our translation). All quotes in this section are from this letter, unless otherwise marked.

2. The term he used here was *Bund* (German: league), referring to the scouting organizations of the German Youth Movement of the early twentieth century, and in this case to Hashomer Hatzair.

3. Monte, Letter 1 (our translation). Most of the letters are undated and they do not appear to be in chronological order.

4. Ibid. (our translation).

5. Jewish citizens of the German Reich had to adopt an additional "Jewish" name starting on January 1, 1939. Monte as a Polish citizen would initially not have been affected by this rule.

6. Monte combined the historical German handwriting Sütterlin with modern Latin cursive script, as was typical at the time.

7. Monte, Letter 4 (our translation).

8. Reg. Nr. 274 068.

9. Karl Monath, Curriculum Vitae, November 1, 1958, private archive of Naomi Baitner.

10. Literally an "*Aasbande*," a gang of rotten carcasses.

11. Monte, Letter 5 (our translation).

12. A quote from the poem "Ulysses" by Alfred Lord Tennyson.

13. Baitner, Interview. After the war, Walter moved to Surfers' Paradise in Queensland, Australia. Reg. Nr. 700 532. The letters also mention Monte's younger cousin Herbert who was set to emigrate to "Erez" (Israel). Monte had written him a letter of recommendation for the Zionist association. Monte, Letter 1 and Letter 4. Herbert eventually went to England with the Kindertransport as well.

14. Monte, Letter 5 (our translation).

15. Monte, Letter 6 (our translation).

16. Government of United Kingdom and Northern Ireland, "Palestine: Statement of Policy," May 23, 1939.

17. Monte, Letter 6 (our translation).

18. Ibid. (our translation).

19. According to the Jewish Address Book of 1931, Ilse Blumenfeld lived and rented rooms at this address. Reg. Nr. 274 068.

20. Monte, Letter 8 (our translation). All further quotes in this section are from this letter, unless otherwise noted.

21. File A.353.075.

22. "Vorbild Flugverkehr," The EMT, www.themt.de/org-1255-49.html. According to Germany's Bundesbank, that has the equivalent purchasing power of 105 euros today. Bundesbank, "Kaufkraftäquivalente historischer Beträge in deutschen Währungen." The price would have represented 1.2 percent of the average annual salary for an individual in Germany in 1939. The same percentage of the average annual salary of 2019 would be closer to 455 euros. Bundesamt für Justiz, *Sozialgesetzbuch (SGB)*, Sechstes Buch (VI), Sechstes Kapitel, Anlage 1, www.gesetze-im-internet.de/sgb_6/anlage_1.html.

23. Original: "det Ding [wird] schon klappen."

24. Bundesamt für Justiz, *Sozialgesetzbuch (SGB)*.

25. Monte, Postcard to Hans Teppich, July 13, 1939, Brussels, private archive of Naomi Baitner (our translation).

26. Monte, Letter 9, Part 1 (our translation). All further quotes in this section are from this letter, unless otherwise marked.

27. This is a quote from the Protestant reformer Ulrich von Hutten (1488–1522). Interestingly, also the title of a book by Udo Voigt, the former president of Germany's neofascist party the National Democratic Party of Germany.

28. Monte, Letter to Karl Monath, undated, probably July 1939, Reg. Nr. 700 532 (our translation). (Letter 10.)

29. Susan Sarah Cohen, ed., *Antisemitism*, volume 17 (Berlin: De Gruyter, 2001), 156–7.

30. Monte, Postcard to Hans Teppich, October 18, 1939, Brussels, private archive of Naomi Baitner.

31. Monte, Letter 9, Part 2 (our translation). All further quotes in this section are from this letter, unless otherwise marked.

32. "Poland to Buy Arms Without Help of Britain," *Chicago Daily Tribune* (Chicago), July 31, 1939.

33. Michael Zalampas, *Adolf Hitler and the Third Reich in American Magazines: 1923–1939* (Bowling Green: Bowling Green State University Popular Press, 1989), 207–8. See also: Helmut Metzmacher, "Deutsch-englische Ausgleichsbemühungen im Sommer 1939," *Vierteljahrshefte für Zeitgeschichte* (München), 14/4 (October 1966), 369–412.

34. Trotsky explained the profound contradiction between German fascism and Russian Stalinism with the example of the division of Poland: "in the territories scheduled to become a part of the USSR, the Moscow government will carry through the expropriation of the large landowners and statification of the means of production. This variant is most probable not because the bureaucracy remains true to the socialist program but because it is neither desirous nor capable of sharing the power, and the privileges the latter entails, with the old ruling classes in the occupied territories. Here an analogy literally offers itself. The first Bonaparte halted the revolution by means of a military dictatorship. However, when the French troops invaded Poland, Napoleon signed a decree: 'Serfdom is abolished'. This measure was dictated not by Napoleon's sympathies for the peasants, nor by democratic principles but rather by the fact that the Bonapartist dictatorship based itself not on feudal, but on bourgeois property relations. Inasmuch as Stalin's Bonapartist dictatorship bases itself not on private but on state property, the invasion of Poland by the Red Army should, in the nature of the case, result in the abolition of private capitalist property, so as thus to bring the regime of the occupied territories into accord with the regime of the USSR. This measure, revolutionary in character – 'the expropriation of the expropriators' – is in this case achieved in a military bureaucratic fashion." Leon Trotsky, "The USSR in War," *New International* (New York), 5/11 (November 1939), 325–32.

35. V.I. Lenin, "Terms of Admission into Communist International," in *Collected Works*, volume 31 (Moscow: Progress Publishers, 1965), 206–11.

36. For the results of this radical break in Comintern policy, see: Jonathan Derrick, *Africa's "Agitators": Militant Anti-Colonialism in Africa and the West 1918-1939* (London: Hurst & Co, 2008).

37. Roy Howard, "Interview with J. Stalin," March 1, 1936, in *Collected Works*, volume 14 (London: Red Star Press, 1978), 133–48.

38. For Trotskyism and Stalinism in the Spanish Civil War, see: Pierre Broué and Emile Temime, *The Revolution and Civil War in Spain* (Chicago: Haymarket Books, 2008); Felix Morrow, *Revolution and Counter Revolution in Spain* (London: New Park Publications, 1963); Leon Trotsky, *The Spanish Revolution 1931–39* (New York: Pathfinder Press, 1973).

39. Karl Monath, CV.

40. Monte, Letter 9, Part 3 (our translation).

41. Ibid. (our translation).

Chapter 4

1. Mandel, "Leon." "Der Autor," in Abraham Leon, *Die jüdische Frage: Eine marxistische Darstellung* (Essen: Arbeiterpresse-Verlag, 1995), 201–8.

2. Abram Leon, *The Jewish Question: A Marxist Interpretation* (Mexico City: Ediciones Pioneras, 1950).

3. Ibid., 211. Mandel summarized this position: "The tragic peculiarities of Jewish society could not be eliminated by seeking to isolate it from decaying society as whole. [...] The world proletarian revolution is alone capable of normalizing Jewish history. Within the framework of decaying capitalism no solution is possible." Mandel, "Leon."

4. Stutje, *Mandel*, 24. Mandel, "Leon."

5. Stutje, *Mandel*, 270, footnote 64.

6. Monte, Postcard to Lotte Teppich, July 29, 1940, Pyrénées-Orientales, private archive of Naomi Baitner (our translation).

7. File A.353.075 (our translation).

8. French and Dutch for "Jew."

9. Monte, Letter 10 (our translation).

10. Sidlof was originally an Austrian citizen, but had been made a German by Germany's *Anschluss* (annexation) of Austria in March 1938.

11. File A.353.075 (our translation).

12. File A.333.563, Justice Ministry, Foreigners' Police, State Archives of Belgium, Brussels.

13. Prager, "Interview," quoted in Segall, "Gestapo" (our translation).

14. Monte, Letter 10 (our translation). This is in reference to Lion Feuchtwanger, *Moskau 1937: Ein Reisebericht für meine Freunde* (Amsterdam: Querido 1937), especially 133–4.

15. It is possible that Leon and Monte knew each other from their time as functionaries of Hashomer Hatzair. In Brussels they also might have shared an apartment, but Stutje does not present any evidence. Stutje, *Mandel*, 25.

16. Lenni Brenner, *Zionism in the Age of the Dictators* (London: Croom Helm, 1983), 180–2.

17. "An End to Zionist Illusions!" *Socialist Appeal* (New York), March 7, 1939.

18. "American Nazi Organization Rally at Madison Square Garden 1939," *Rare Historical Photos*, February 19, 2014, http://rarehistoricalphotos.com/american-nazi-organization-rally-madison-square-garden-1939/.

19. Brenner, *Zionism*, 182.

20. Many Trotskyists came from Hashomer Hatzair. We have already seen the development of Leon and Viktor in Brussels, as well as that of Segall and Moneta in Haifa in the second half of the 1930s. Moshé Machover was a founder of the Trotskyist organization Matzpen in Israel in 1962 – he too had previously been expelled from Hashomer Hatzair. Dov Shas fought in the resistance against the German occupation in Romania, and moved to Palestine with Hashomer Hatzair after the war. He worked at the Haifa oil refinery, and his desire for Jewish-Arab workers' unity led him to break with left Zionism and join the Trotskyist group around Jakob Taut, who later also became part of Matzpen. Fiedler, *Matzpen*, 41, 101.

Upon more careful examination, the list of Trotskyists who began their political life in Hashomer Hatzair is enormous: Baruch Hirson (1921–99, South Africa), Boris Fraenkel (1921–2006, Switzerland and France), Chanie Rosenberg (1922–, Palestine and Britain), Henri Weber (1944–, France), and Christian Picquet (1952–, France). Leopold Trepper (1904–82) went from Hashomer Hatzair to official Communism, yet expressed sympathies for Trotskyism at the end of his life.

21. Karl Kautsky, the leading theoretician of the Second International, wrote in 1914: "The International is incapable of preventing [war] [...] it is not a useful instrument in war; it is fundamentally an instrument for peace." Quoted in *Illustrierte Geschichte der deutschen Revolution* (Berlin: Internationaler Arbeiter-Verlag, 1929), 114 (our translation). This idea was rejected by Rosa Luxemburg, and this rejection had been a founding principle of the Third and later the Fourth International.

22. Leon Trotsky, "Imperialist War and the Proletarian World Revolution," *Socialist Appeal* (New York), June 29, 1940.

23. "Organizational Report of the IKD," in *International Bulletin: Information Service of the 4th Int'l* (New York), 1/1 (July 1940).

24. Wolfgang Alles, *Zur Politik und Geschichte der deutschen Trotzkisten ab 1930* (Cologne: Neuer ISP Verlag, 1987), 256–7, 268–71.

25. For the group in Denmark, see: "Jungclas, Georg," in Hermann Weber and Andreas Herbst, eds., *Deutsche Kommunisten: Biographisches Handbuch 1918 bis 1945* (Berlin: Dietz Verlag, 2008), 421; Ernest Mandel, "Georg Jungclas," *Revue Quatrième Internationale* (Paris), 22 (Autumn 1975), English translation published at www.revolutionaryhistory.co.uk but website not currently functioning. For the group in Belgium, see: Gertjan Desme, "'Eine kostbare Kette standhafter Revolutionäre': De Internationale Kommunisten Deutschlands in Antwerpen en Brussel (1933–1940)," in *Journal of Belgian History* (Brussels), 45/2–3 (2015), 80–119. For a German Trotskyist who survived the war in Berlin-Charlottenburg, see: Oskar Hippe, *... And Red is the Colour of Our Flag: Memories of Sixty Years*

in the Workers' Movement (London: Index Books, 1991). Alexander, *Trotsky-ism*, 427–9.

26. Rodolphe Prager, "The Fourth International during the Second World War," *Revolutionary History* (London), 1/3 (Autumn 1988). Prager was not just a historian, but also an active member of the Fourth International in France during the war. Alexander, *Trotskyism*, 297–8. "Theses on the Liquidation of World War II and the Revolutionary Upsurge, *Fourth International* (New York), 6/3 (March 1945), 78–86, and 6/5 (May 1945), 150–2.

27. Ibid.

28. Segall, "Gestapo."

29. Alles, *Trotzkisten*, 275. This league also produced a single issue of the hec-tographed bulletin *Unser Wort* (German: Our Word) in June 1944. The issue consists solely of the "Theses on the Liquidation of World War II and the Revolutionary Upsurge" which were passed by the European confer-ence of the Fourth International in February of that year. This publication is preserved in the library of the Friedrich-Ebert-Stiftung in Bonn.

30. Karl Liebknecht, "Der Hauptfeind steht im eigenen Land!" *Ausgewählte Reden und Aufsätze* (Berlin: Dietz Verlag, 1952), 296–301, English trans-lation at the Marxists Internet Archive, "The Main Enemy is at Home!" www.marxists.org/archive/liebknecht-k/works/1915/05/main-enemy-home.htm.

31. In the Second World War, the Trotskyists were opposed to all imperial-ist powers but gave critical support to the Soviet Union. They defended the social gains of the October Revolution (the nationalized property of the means of production, the monopoly of foreign trade, etc.) against capitalist incursions. Yet they remained hostile to the bureaucratic caste under Stalin which undermined the proletarian relations of production. In a similar sense, the Trotskyists also gave critical solidarity to the inde-pendence movements in the colonies. While the imperialist powers were waging a reactionary war of conquest, the independence of the colonized countries was a historically progressive task. Trotsky, "Imperialist War."

The Second World War, moreover, posed a series of new problems that had not been present during the First World War, namely a greater combination of different types of wars within the framework of an interimperialist conflict, such as (1) wars for national liberation by nations oppressed by both sides, in different continents, which had barely been observed in the first war; (2) the existence of the USSR, a bureaucratized workers' state, as one of the warring countries; and (3) Germany's military occupation of other imperialist countries, some of them of the first tier, such as France or later Italy. For this reason, Trotsky proposed a special policy for the workers of the "democratic" imperialist countries threat-ened by the Nazis' advance: the "proletarian military policy." According to

Trotsky, the workers of these countries should not leave the defense against Nazi occupation in the hands of bourgeois politicians and generals, such as Marshal Pétain of France, who established a German puppet regime. Trotsky proposed that the trade unions and workers' organizations independently organize military instruction, enlistment and combat. Socialist Workers Party, "Resolution on Proletarian Military Policy," September 27, 1940, *Prometheus Research Series* (New York), 2 (1989).

32. This was the analysis of Viktor and the Trotskyists. See the lead article of the first number of *Arbeiter und Soldat*.

33. Ministère des Affaires Étrangères, *The French Yellow Book: Diplomatic Documents (1938–1939)* (New York: Reynal & Hitchcock, 1940), 304.

34. Bodo Scheurig, *Verräter oder Patrioten: Das Nationalkomitee "Freies Deutschland" und der Bund Deutscher Offiziere in der Sowjetunion 1943–1945* (Berlin: Propyläen Verlag, 1993), 45.

35. Craipeau, *Swimming,* 140.

36. "Pas de Chauvinisme dans les Rangs Ouvriers!" *La Vérité* (Paris), January 20, 1942 (our translation).

37. Breitman, "Gestapo."

38. Calvès, *Sans bottes* (our translation)

39. Ibid. (our translation).

40. Paul Thalmann, Letter to Jakob Moneta, January 13, 1970, Rodolphe Prager papers, folder 301, IISG, Amsterdam. (Letter 1.)

41. Calvès, *Sans bottes*. "DCA" stands for "défense contre avions."

42. Quoted in "Proletaires de tous les pays, unissez-vous! Proleten aller Laender, vereinigt euch!" *La Verité* (Paris), October 15, 1943 (translation from Craipeau, *Swimming,* 245).

43. Ibid. (translation from Craipeau).

44. *Zeitung für Soldat und Arbeiter im Westen* (Brest), 2 (reprinted in Brabant, *Fac-simile,* 198) (our translation).

45. He used the German term *Kamerad,* which was used for fellow soldiers, in contrast to the more socialist term *Genosse,* which is equivalent to the English "comrade."

46. Ibid. (our translation).

47. Ibid. (our translation).

48. Calvès, *Sans bottes* (our translation).

49. Leon Trotsky, "Man Does Not Live by Politics Alone," *Labour Monthly* (London) 5/5 (November 1923).

50. Thalmann, *Revolution,* 334–5 (our translation).

51. Ibid. (our translation).

52. Ibid., 293–4, 334. The address can be found in Paul Thalmann's two letters to Jakob Moneta. Thalmann wrote in his autobiography that Viktor was with them "with short interruptions until March of 1944"

(our translation). This seems very unlikely since Viktor fled to Belgium in October of 1943 and Thalmann does not seem to know anything about his activities after this time. The Rue Friant is just 600 meters from the Rue Marie Rose where Lenin lived from 1909 to 1911. "Lenin's Anonymous (and Loving) Stay in the 14th Arrondissement," *Un jour de plus à Paris*, January 6, 1917, www.unjourdeplusaparis.com/en/paris-reportage/lenine-14e-arrondissement-paris.

53. Ibid., 294 (our translation).

54. Are Thalmann's recollections always credible? We will investigate this in Section 5.4.

55. Ibid., 316 (our translation).

56. Ibid. (our translation).

57. Thalmann, Letter 1 (our translation).

58. David Broder, "Trotskyism in Occupied France," *Workers Liberty* (London), 3/20 (June 2008), 2.

59. "Germany is the lynchpin and the fulcrum of the world revolution. Only German revolution is world revolution. Yet the German proletariat is still the weakest and most inactive in the world." Karl Liebknecht, "Die Frage des Tages," *Reden und Aufsätze* (Hamburg: Verlag der Kommunistischen Internationale, 1921), 315 (our translation).

60. Alexander Rabinowitch, *The Bolsheviks Come to Power: The Revolution of 1917 in Petrograd* (New York: W.W. Norton, 1976), 72–4.

61. Lenin called Marxism "a summing up of experience, illuminated by a profound philosophical conception of the world and a rich knowledge of history." V.I. Lenin, *The State and Revolution*, in *Selected Works*, volume 2 (New York: International Publishers, 1968), 282.

62. "Manifesto of the Fourth International on the Dissolution of the Comintern," *Fourth International* (New York), 4/7 (July 1943).

63. Thalmann, *Revolution*, 335 (our translation).

64. Quoted in Craipeau, *Swimming*, 143.

65. Calvès, *Sans bottes* (our translation).

Chapter 5

1. Ibid. (our translation). The date is not included in Calvès memoirs. It can be found in Craipeau, *Swimming*, 245.

2. Ibid. (our translation). The name of André Calvès' younger brother is provided by his son Michel Calvès, son of André, e-mail message to author, August 22, 2017.

3. *Amtliches Fernsprechbuch Hamburg*, editions from 1969–80. There are also entries for a "K. Leplow" in Hamburg address books around 1940.

4. "Frank," interview with the author, March 27, 2017 (our translation). "Frank's identity is known to the author but he wishes to remain anonymous.

5. Such plans might sound astounding, given Trotskyism's critical attitude toward individual terrorism. However, in the 1970s, the United Secretariat of the Fourth International – the international organization of the LCR and the GIM – was enthusiastic about the guerrilla strategy. This enthusiasm was not limited to lectures by Ernest Mandel on the necessity of armed struggle, such as the one he gave at the Vietnam Congress in Berlin in February of 1968. Sections of the United Secretariat participated in and even founded guerrilla groups. The Revolutionary Workers Party – The Combatant (PRT-El Combatiente) in Argentina, the Revolutionary Workers Party – Combat (POR-Combate) in Bolivia, or the Revolutionary Communist League (LKI) in the Basque Country were all involved in robberies, kidnappings, and armed battles against the state at this time. The Hamburg GIM also had internal discussions in this direction: Members like Christa Eckes or Wolfgang Beer (the former in the GIM's Central Committee) later joined the Red Army Faction. Yet Hans-Jürgen Schulz, the leader of the Hamburg Trotskyists for many years, ensured that the GIM kept its distance from guerrilla actions. "Max," interview with the author, March 25, 2017. "Max's" identity is known to the author but he wishes to remain anonymous.

6. Craipeau, *Swimming*, 245.

7. Ibid.; Thalmann, Revolution, 336; Cobb, Resistance, 210–11.

8. There is also no file for Konrad Leplow. Christine Botzet (Federal Archive of Germany, Military Archive Department), e-mail message to author, November 29, 2016. The same applies to the archives in Prague, where files of the Reich Court Marshall are also preserved. Josef Žikeš (Military Central Archives of the Czech Republic), e-mail message to author, April 12, 2017.

9. Craipeau, *Swimming*, 245.

10. "La Gestapo pourchasse nos militants," *La Vérité* (Paris), October 15, 1943 (translation from Craipeau, *Swimming*, 245).

11. Craipeau, *Swimming*, 245.

12. "Proletaires de tous les pays, unissez-vous! Proleten aller Laender, vereinigt euch!" *La Verité* (Paris), October 15, 1943.

13. Calvés (our translation).

14. "La Gestapo pourchasse nos militants', *La Vérité* (Paris), October 15, 1943 (translation from Craipeau, *Swimming*, 245).

15. Segall, "Gestapo."

16. Prager, "Fourth International."

17. Craipeau, *Swimming*, 143.

18. Heinz Abosch, *Flucht ohne Heimkehr: Aus dem Leben eines Heimatlosen* (Stuttgart: Radius, 1997), 86–9, 123–7 (our translation).

19. Rodolphe Prager, "HIRZEL Paul, dit Kast, dit Rémont, dit Paul. Nom d'emprunt de Nathan W." *Le Maitron: Dictionnaire Biographique Mouvement Ouvrier Mouvement Social*, April 22, 2010, http://maitron-en-ligne.univ-paris1.fr/spip.php?article87671.

20. This issue makes references to the assassination attempt on Hitler from July 20, 1944, and therefore must have been at least partially written after Viktor's arrest. The orthography of this issue is also noticeably worse than the others, with numerous French spellings (Moscou, Staline, Fonction-ary) and commas placed almost at random.

21. Christine Heymann, Letter to an unknown recipient, presumably Rodolphe Prager, May 17, 1977, Rodolphe Prager papers, folder 301, IISG, Amsterdam.

22. Mathias Corvin was, alongside Fred Zeller, a leading member of the Revolutionary Socialist Youth (JSR) who merged with the Trotskyists in 1936. In November 1937, both were expelled from the Internationalist Workers Party (POI), but later reinstated. After the war, Corvin, together with Lucienne Abraham (Michèle Mestre), became a leader of the Pabloist faction within Trotskyism. Corvin and Mestre left the Fourth International in 1954 and joined the French Communist Party (PCF). Even later they became followers of Mao.

23. Heymann, Letter (our translation).

24. Spoulber, wounded, made it to the apartment of Fred Zeller. This is noted in a different handwriting on the margins of the letter, and confirmed by Prager in "Fourth International."

25. Thalmann, *Revolution*, 338 (our translation).

26. Heymann, Letter (our translation).

27. Baget, "Nous accusons" (our translation). This obituary is signed by Marguerite Baget, which was probably a pseudonym for Heymann. Heymann reported in her letter that she had not written the article "personally and I can hardly remember it either." We can assume that the obituary was drafted by an anonymous Trotskyist editor on the basis of a conversation with Heymann shortly after her return. It is quite possible that in 1946 she remembered the dates of her arrest more precisely than in 1977. Yet the content of this article is problematic as well. Viktor's career in the Zionist movement is completely ignored. There is talk of a "virtual liaison network among the various revolutionary cells spread across Germany and Austria" during the Second World War – and according to the information now available, this is quite exaggerated.

28. Thalmann, *Revolution*, 338 (our translation).

29. Thalmann, *Revolution*, 338–43. The following account is from Thalmann's memoirs. The date of Thalmann's visit is from: Rudolf Segall, Letter to an unknown recipient, December 21, 1989, Rodolphe Prager papers, folder 301, IISG, Amsterdam.

30. Is Thalmann's account credible? We will investigate this question in Chapter 5.4.

31. This scene is only in the European version of the film. *Brazil* (1985), alternate versions, IMDB, www.imdb.com/title/tt0088846/alternateversions.

32. Prager, "Fourth International."

33. Philippe Bourrinet, "MONATH Martin, dit WITTLIN, Paul WIDELIN, Paul WENTELEY, VICTOR," *Le Maitron: Dictionnaire Biographique Mouvement Ouvrier Mouvement Social*, January 15, 2019, http://maitron-en-ligne.univ-paris1.fr/spip.php?article168946.

34. Beschluss, Martin Ludwig Witlin (früher: Monath), Bestand B Rep. 042 (Todeserklärungen), Amtsgericht Charlottenburg, Archive of the *Land* Berlin.

35. Reg. Nr. 700 532.

36. Thalmann, *Revolution*, 335 (our translation).

37. Thalmann, Letter 1 (our translation).

38. Paul Thalmann, Letter to Jakob Moneta. June 24, 1970, Rodolphe Prager papers, folder 301, IISG, Amsterdam (our translation). (Letter 2.)

39. Ibid. (our translation).

40. Thalmann, Letter 1 (our translation).

41. Ibid. (our translation).

42. Segall, Letter.

43. "Bericht über die Beziehungen zwischen den R.K. (Spartakusbewegung) und der deutschen Sektion der 4. Internationale (Bolschewiken-Leninisten)," Paris, October 13, 1947, Georg Scheuer papers, document 353, IISG, Amsterdam (our translation). Thanks to Peter Berens for this reference. Ignaz Duhl was a member of the RKD who was murdered by the Gestapo in 1943 in Marseille.

Chapter 6

1. Antonio Gramsci, *Selections from the Prison Notebooks* (New York: International Publishers, 1972), 153.

2. Leon Trotsky, "Once Again, Whither France?," in *Leon Trotsky on France* (New York: Monad Press, 1979), 70.

3. Mandel, "Leon."

4. Klaus-Michael Mallmann and Martin Cüppers, *Halbmond und Hakenkreuz: Das Dritte Reich, die Araber und Palästina* (Darmstadt: Wissenschaftliche

Buchgesellschaft, 2006). See also: Jakob Taut, *Judenfrage und Zionismus* (Cologne: Neuer ISP Verlag, 1986).

5. Nachman Ben-Yehuda, *The Masada Myth: Collective Memory and Myth-making in Israel* (Madison: University of Wisconsin Press, 1996), 132–5. "Masada" is a reference to the 960 Jews who were besieged by a Roman legion in 73 BC in the Masada fortress on the Dead Sea. Rather than surrendering, they chose collective suicide – or so the legend goes.

Bibliography

Archives

Archive of the *Land* Berlin *[Berliner Landesarchiv]*, Berlin.

Reparations Office *[Entschädigungsbehörde]*, Berlin.

International Institute of Social History (IISG), Amsterdam:

– Rodolphe Prager Papers, Folder 301 (Martin Monat).

– Rodolphe Prager Papers, Folder 290 (Ernest Mandel).

– Georg Scheuer Papers.

Main Archive of the *Land* Brandenburg *[Brandenburgisches Landeshauptarchiv]*, Potsdam.

Private archive of Naomi Baitner, Rehovot.

State Archives of Belgium, Brussels.

Newspapers

Arbeiter und Soldat [Paris, 1943–4], reprinted in Jean-Michel Brabant, ed., *Fac-simile de "La Vérité" clandestine: 1940–1944* (Paris: ÉDI, 1978).

Hashomer Hatzair [Warsaw, 1927–39], available at http://web.nli.org.il/sites/JPress/Hebrew/Pages/HAS.aspx.

Socialist Appeal [New York, 1935–41], available at www.marxists.org/history/etol/newspape/socialistappeal/index.htm.

Unser Wort [Paris, 1944], available at the library of the Friedrich-Ebert-Stiftung, Bonn.

La Verite [Paris, 1940–4], reprinted in Brabant, *Fac-simile*.

Zeitung für Arbeiter und Soldat im Westen [Brest, 1943], reprinted in Brabant, Facsimile.

Books and Pamphlets

Wolfgang Abendroth, *Einführung in die Geschichte der Arbeiterbewegung: Band I* (Heilbronn: Distel, 1985).

Heinz Abosch, *Flucht ohne Heimkehr: Aus dem Leben eines Heimatlosen* (Stuttgart: Radius, 1997).

Robert J. Alexander, *International Trotskyism* (Durham, NC: Duke University Press, 1991).

Bibliography

Wolfgang Alles, *Zur Politik und Geschichte der deutschen Trotzkisten ab 1930* (Cologne: Neuer ISP Verlag, 1987).

Carina Baganz, *Diskriminierung, Ausgrenzung, Vertreibung: Die Technische Hochschule Berlin während des Nationalsozialismus* (Berlin: Metropol, 2013).

Joel Beinin, *Was the Red Flag Flying There? Marxist Politics and the Arab-Israeli Conflict in Egypt and Israel, 1948–1965* (Berkeley: University of California Press, 1990).

Nachman Ben-Yehuda, *The Masada Myth: Collective Memory and Mythmaking in Israel* (Madison: University of Wisconsin Press, 1996).

Peter Berens, *Trotzkisten gegen Hitler* (Cologne: Neuer ISP Verlag, 2007).

Alina Bothe and Gertrud Pickhan, eds., *Ausgewiesen! Berlin, 28.10.1938: Die Geschichte der "Polenaktion"* (Berlin: Metropol, 2018).

Lenni Brenner, *Zionism in the Age of the Dictators* (London: Croom Helm, 1983).

Pierre Broué and Emile Temime, *The Revolution and Civil War in Spain* (Chicago: Haymarket Books, 2008).

André Calvès, *Sans bottes ni médailles: Un trotskyste breton dans la guerre* (Montreuil: Editions La Brèche, 1984).

Matthew Cobb, *The Resistance: The French Fight Against the Nazis* (London: Simon & Schuster, 2009).

Susan Sarah Cohen, ed., *Antisemitism*, volume 17 (Berlin: De Gruyter, 2001).

Yvan Craipeau, *Swimming Against the Tide: Trotskyists in German Occupied France* (London: Merlin Press, 2012).

Jonathan Derrick, *Africa's "Agitators": Militant Anti-Colonialism in Africa and the West 1918–1939* (London: Hurst & Co, 2008).

Suska Döpp, *Jüdische Jugendbewegung in Köln 1906–1938* (Münster: LIT Verlag, 1997).

Lion Feuchtwanger, *Moskau 1937: Ein Reisebericht für meine Freunde* (Amsterdam: Querido, 1937).

Lutz Fiedler, *Matzpen: Eine andere israelische Geschichte* (Göttingen: Vandenhoeck & Ruprecht, 2017).

Paul Frölich, *Im radikalen Lager: Politische Autobiographie 1890–1921* (Berlin: Basisdruck, 2013).

Adolfo Gilly, *La Revolución Interrumpida* (México: Ediciones El Caballito, 1971).

Antonio Gramsci, *Selections from the Prison Notebooks* (New York: International Publishers, 1972).

Raphael Gross, *November 1938: Die Katastrophe vor der Katastrophe* (Munich: C.H. Beck, 2013).

Oskar Hippe, *… And Red is the Colour of Our Flag: Memories of Sixty Years in the Workers' Movement* (London: Index Books, 1991).

Ralf Hoffrogge, *A Jewish Communist in Weimar Germany: The Life of Werner Scholem (1895–1940)* (Leiden: Brill, 2017).

Ralf Hoffrogge, *Working-Class Politics in the German Revolution: Richard Müller, the Revolutionary Shop Stewards and the Origins of the Council Movement* (Leiden: Brill, 2014).

V.I. Lenin, *The State and Revolution*, in *Selected Works*, volume 2 (New York: International Publishers, 1968).

Abram Leon, *The Jewish Question: A Marxist Interpretation* (Mexico City: Ediciones Pioneras, 1950).

Klaus-Michael Mallmann and Martin Cüppers, *Halbmond und Hakenkreuz: Das Dritte Reich, die Araber und Palästina* (Darmstadt: Wissenschaftliche Buchgesellschaft, 2006).

Rafael Medoff, *Historical Dictionary of Zionism* (New York: Routledge, 2012).

Ministère des Affaires Étrangères, *The French Yellow Book: Diplomatic Documents (1938–1939)* (New York: Reynal & Hitchcock, 1940).

Felix Morrow, *Revolution and Counter Revolution in Spain* (London: New Park Publications, 1963).

Alexander Rabinowitch, *The Bolsheviks Come to Power: The Revolution of 1917 in Petrograd* (New York: W.W. Norton, 1976).

Alfred Rosenberg, *Die Spur des Juden im Wandel der Zeit* (Munich: Zentralverlag der NSDAP, 1937).

Annegret Schüle, *Trotzkismus in Deutschland bis 1933: "Für die Arbeitereinheitsfront zur Abwehr des Faschismus"* (Cologne: Self-published, 1989).

Jan Willem Stutje, *Ernest Mandel: A Rebel's Dream Deferred* (London: Verso, 2009).

Jakob Taut, *Judenfrage und Zionismus* (Cologne: Neuer ISP Verlag, 1986).

Clara and Paul Thalmann, *Revolution für die Freiheit: Stationen eines politischen Kampfes Moskau/Madrid/Paris* (Hamburg: Verlag Association, 1977).

Leon Trotsky, *Leon Trotsky on France* (New York: Monad Press, 1979).

Leon Trotsky, *The Spanish Revolution 1931–39* (New York: Pathfinder Press, 1973).

Leon Trotsky, *Trotsky's Diary in Exile: 1935* (London: Faber and Faber, 1958).

Susanne Urban, ed., *"Rettet die Kinder!" Die Jugend-Aliyah 1933 bis 2003: Einwanderung und Jugendarbeit in Israel* (Frankfurt/Main: Kinder- und Jugend-Aliyah Deutschland, 2003).

Hermann Weber and Andreas Herbst, eds., *Deutsche Kommunisten: Biographisches Handbuch 1918 bis 1945* (Berlin: Dietz Verlag, 2008).

Michael Zalampas, *Adolf Hitler and the Third Reich in American Magazines: 1923–1939* (Bowling Green: Bowling Green State University Popular Press, 1989).

Illustrierte Geschichte der deutschen Revolution (Berlin: Internationaler Arbeiter-Verlag, 1929).

Online Databases

Bundesarchiv, *Gedenkbuch*, www.bundesarchiv.de/gedenkbuch.

Lubitz' TrotskyanaNet, "Name Authority Files," www.trotskyana.net/Trotskyists/NameFiles/namefiles.html.

Staats- und Universitätsbibliothek Hamburg, *Amtliches Fernsprechbuch Hamburg*, http://agora.sub.uni-hamburg.de/subhh-adress/digbib/start.

Yad Vashem, Central Database of Shoah Victims' Names, http://yvng.yadvashem.org.

Zentral und Landesbibliothek Berlin, *Berliner Adressbücher 1799 bis 1943*, www.zlb.de/besondere-angebote/berliner-adressbuecher.html.

Articles, Documents, and Other Resources

Wolfgang Alles, "Cyrano von Bergerac und die Geduld des Revolutionärs" (Interview with Rudolf Segall), *Inprekorr* (Cologne), 414/415 and 416/417 (May/June and July/August 2006).

"American Nazi Organization Rally at Madison Square Garden 1939," *Rare Historical Photos*, February 19, 2014, http://rarehistoricalphotos.com/american-nazi-organization-rally-madison-square-garden-1939/.

Eli Ashkenazi, "Hashomer Hatzair Youth Movement Comes Full Circle With Relaunch in Germany," *Ha'aretz* (Tel Aviv), October 9, 2011.

Brazil (1985), alternate versions, IMDB, www.imdb.com/title/tt0088846/alternateversions.

David Broder, "Trotskyism in Occupied France," *Workers Liberty* (London), 3/20 (June 2008), 2.

Pierre Broué, "In Germany for the International," *Revolutionary History*, 9/4 (2008).

André Calvès, "La trahison de Conrad Leplow Octobre 1943," manuscript in the BDIC in Paris, probably from 1944, http://andre-calves.org/autres%20redactions/La%20trahison%20de%20Conrad%20LEPLOW%20octobre%201943.htm.

Winston Churchill, "Zionism versus Bolshevism," *Illustrated Sunday Herald* (London), February 8, 1920.

"Der Autor," in Abraham Leon, *Die jüdische Frage: Eine marxistische Darstellung* (Essen: Arbeiterpresse-Verlag 1995), 201–8.

Gertjan Desme, "'Eine kostbare Kette standhafter Revolutionäre': De Internationale Kommunisten Deutschlands in Antwerpen en Brussel (1933–1940)," *Journal of Belgian History* (Brussels), 45/2–3 (2015), 80–119.

"Geschichte der Nürtingen-Grundschule," www.nuertingen-grundschule.de/schulweb/geschichte-der-schule.html.

Wladek Flakin, "Hinter der Bühne der Revolte," *Klasse Gegen Klasse* (Berlin), 6 (April 2013).

Fritz Hermann, "Jakob Moneta: Interview zum achtzigsten Geburtstag," *Inprekorr* (Cologne), 278 (December 1994).

Ralf Hoffrogge, "Der Sommer des Nationalbolschewismus? Die Stellung der KPD-Linken zum Ruhrkampf und ihre Kritik am 'Schlageter-Kurs' von 1923," *Sozial.Geschichte Online* (Duisburg-Essen), 20 (2017), 99–146.

Gerhard Hanloser, "Die Rote Fahne und der Antisemitismus: Olaf Kistenmachers Präsentation tatsächlicher und vermeintlicher antijüdischer Aussagen in der KPD-Tageszeitung," *Sozial.Geschichte Online* (Duisburg-Essen), 20 (2017), 175–96.

Government of United Kingdom and Northern Ireland, "Palestine: Statement of Policy," May 23, 1939.

"Jakob Moneta wird 85," *Avanti* (Cologne), 44 (November 1999).

Daniel Kahn and Oy Division, "Oy Ir Narishe Tsienistn / Oh You Foolish Little Zionists / Глупые Сионисты," www.haggadot.com/clip/lyrics-oy-ir-narishe-tsienistn-oh-you-foolish-little-zionists-глупые-сионисты.

V.I. Lenin, "Terms of Admission into Communist International," in *Collected Works*, volume 31 (Moscow: Progress Publishers, 1965), 206–11.

"Lenin's Anonymous (and Loving) Stay in the 14th Arrondissement," *Un jour de plus à Paris*, January 6, 1917, www.unjourdeplusaparis.com/en/paris-reportage/lenine-14e-arrondissement-paris.

Karl Liebknecht, "Die Frage des Tages," *Reden und Aufsätze* (Hamburg: Verlag der Kommunistischen Internationale, 1921), 315.

Karl Liebknecht, "Der Hauptfeind steht im eigenen Land!" *Ausgewählte Reden und Aufsätze* (Berlin: Dietz Verlag, 1952), 296–301; English translation at the Marxists Internet Archive, "The Main Enemy is at Home!" www.marxists.org/archive/liebknecht-k/works/1915/05/main-enemy-home.htm.

"Manifesto of the Fourth International on the Dissolution of the Comintern," *Fourth International* (New York), 4/7 (July 1943).

Ernest Mandel [Germain], "A. Leon," *Fourth International* (New York), 8/6 (June 1947), 172–6.

Ernest Mandel, "Georg Jungclas,' *Revue Quatrième Internationale* (Paris), 22 (Autumn 1975).

Helmut Metzmacher, "Deutsch-englische Ausgleichsbemühungen im Sommer 1939," *Vierteljahrshefte für Zeitgeschichte* (München), 14/4 (October 1966), 369–412.

"Michael Pablo," *Cahiers Leon Trotsky*, 57 (March 1996), 120.

"Organizational Report of the IKD," in *International Bulletin: Information Service of the 4th Int'l* (New York), 1/1 (July 1940).

Ernst Piper, "Als der 1. Mai braun wurde," *Spiegel Online*, Einestages, April 30, 2008.

"Poland to Buy Arms Without Help of Britain," *Chicago Daily Tribune* (Chicago), July 31, 1939.

Rodolphe Prager, "The Fourth International during the Second World War," *Revolutionary History* (London), 1/3 (Autumn 1988).

Rodolphe Prager, "HIRZEL Paul, dit Kast, dit Rémont, dit Paul. Nom d'emprunt de Nathan W." *Le Maitron: Dictionnaire Biographique Mouvement Ouvrier Mouvement Social*, April 22, 2010, http://maitron-en-ligne.univ-paris1.fr/spip.php?article87671.

Bodo Scheurig, *Verräter oder Patrioten: Das Nationalkomitee "Freies Deutschland" und der Bund Deutscher Offiziere in der Sowjetunion 1943–1945* (Berlin: Propyläen Verlag, 1993).

Rudolf Segall, "'Die Gestapo hat mich erschossen': Leben und Tod eines deutsch-jüdischen Widerstandskämpfers," *Bresche* (Zurich), 89/11 (1989), 31–4.

Socialist Workers Party, "Resolution on Proletarian Military Policy," September 27, 1940, *Prometheus Research Series* (New York), 2 (1989).

"Theses on the Liquidation of World War II and the Revolutionary Upsurge," *Fourth International* (New York), 6/3 (March 1945), 78–86, and 6/5 (May 1945), 150–2.

Leon Trotsky, "German Perspectives," *Class Struggle* (New York), 3/9 and 3/10 (October 1933 and November 1933).

Leon Trotsky, "Imperialist War and the Proletarian World Revolution," *Socialist Appeal* (New York), June 29, 1940.

Leon Trotsky, "Man Does Not Live by Politics Alone," *Labour Monthly* (London), 5/5 (November 1923).

Leon Trotsky, "The USSR in War," *New International* (New York), 5/11 (November 1939), 325–32.

Leon Trotsky, "Why Marxists Oppose Individual Terrorism," originally published in German in *Der Kampf* (Vienna), November 1911, English translation from the Marxists Internet Archive, www.marxists.org/archive/trotsky/1911/11/tia09.htm.

"Vorbild Flugverkehr," The EMT, www.themt.de/org-1255–49.html.

PART II

WORKER AND SOLDIER

Worker and Soldier: Notes on Translation

Arbeiter und Soldat was not a well-written newspaper. To be more precise: The writing was full of revolutionary fervor and sharp analysis, but the extreme repression did not allow for good editing or proofreading. The letters written by German soldiers are particularly clunky. Previous translations of the newspaper (in French and English) smoothed out the text. This translation, in contrast, tries to recreate the original reading experience, complete with typos, repeated terms, and run-on sentences.

The 1944 issues were made by a French typesetter and lack German letters like ä, ö, ü, and ß. The final issue – completed after Martin Monath's arrest – was apparently not proofread by a native speaker. Numerous French spellings appear: "Moskau" becomes "Moscou," "Stalin" "Staline," and "Funktionär" "Fonctionär." All these mistakes have been translated as far as possible and are not marked.

The issues are not perfectly preserved, and only scraps remain of the 1943 soldiers' newspaper. Illegible passages are marked with [...]. This translation was based on David Broder's 2008 translation from French to English, but very extensively revised based on the original German. Thanks to comrade Broder for permission to use this.

Nathaniel Flakin

The German Revolution is the World Revolution.
K. Liebknecht

WORKER and SOLDIER

Organ for proletarian-revolutionary unification
No. 1
July 1943

WHAT DOES WORKER AND SOLDIER STAND FOR?

Are we facing a proletarian revolution?

Once again the specter of communist revolution is haunting the globe. In Germany Goering invites his *Volksgenossen* ["national comrades"] from S.S. and Gestapo to punch German workers in the face if they express their thoughts about the coming proletarian revolution. Göbbels writes: "this war is already the social revolution." He uses incantations like this in an attempt to dispel his fear of the revolution which has now become inevitable. In England even the Conservatives, hoping to calm the proletarian fermentation, are talking of projects to improve the well-being of the people after the war. In America high finance warns: "If Stalin goes back to Trotsky's doctrine of international revolution" – or, more precisely, if communist revolution breaks out – "we will smother it with war." In the name of the capitalists of America and the whole world, Roosevelt calls on Stalin to dissolve the Third International. In Russia – yes in Russia – the Stalin clique indeed dissolves the International. The Russian bosses cry out for revenge against the German people, and they are making every effort to prove to their dear allies their honorable intention to nip any communist revolution in the bud.

This is how these gentlemen view the danger of communist revolution, and this is how they are preparing to greet it. But what about the workers, the countless hundreds of millions of exploited people? Most importantly, what about the German proletariat? Is communist revolution really around the corner, or is the ruling class just seeing ghosts when it looks at the bloodbath of peoples it has organized for its profits?

We must pose the question even more sharply. These gentlemen would have no objection to an upheaval in Germany which would take power from the Hitler clique and bring victory for the Anglo-Saxon imperialists. On the contrary. This is why working-class districts are bombed day and night, with the aim of heightening bitterness and thus pushing the desperate masses to revolt. An uprising is certainly part of these heroes' program, as long as it brings a dictator to power or, in the worst case, some sort of "democratic" government which would be required to comply with the wishes of Anglo-American capital.[1]

But revolutions mean that the ground will get hot and unstable beneath their feet. Once millions of workers are on the march, they may not stop until they have reached their own goal, creating a republic of councils as the foundation for building socialism. But doesn't everything suggest that the wishes of the gentlemen in Washington, London, and Moscow will be fulfilled? Didn't the German proletariat let its revolution slip through its fingers once already? Haven't Himmler's terror and Göbbels' stupefying propaganda broken the German working class for decades and completely destroyed its faith in its own revolutionary strength? Can we even picture the European revolution going beyond the tight limits set by the Anglo-Saxon imperialists? That is the question.

Have we progressed since 1918?

The revolution of 1918 failed mainly because of three shortcomings. First and second: millions of working people were still full of illusions in the capitalist system and the democratic republic. Third: millions of working people who wanted to fight for socialism still trusted the old Social Democratic Party which had long since degenerated and whose bosses only had one thing in mind: to pass the power that had been entrusted to them into the hands of the bourgeoisie, to disarm the proletariat and remove the main instruments of revolution, the workers' and soldiers' councils.

The fact that millions of working people expected capitalism to improve their living conditions can be explained because until the World War, the capitalist system was still on the rise. This period ended decisively at that time. Post-war crisis, inflation, a short recovery but still a million workers in Germany unemployed; then the deep crisis in which almost eight million are on the dole; resulting from this, under Nazi rule, the rearmament boom as the only solution to the crisis but inevitably leading to war; all this has liberated the working class from a host of illusions in the capitalist system.

Much the same happened with the democratic illusions. The "democratic republic" was built on the points of bayonets directed against the working class. Instead of rifles and councils, the workers were given ballot papers, the Reichswehr and protective custody [detention without trial]. Their leaders were bribed with the capitalists' funds, ministerial posts, or little jobs in the unions, blocking every step toward a revolutionary solution. In the crisis, "democracy" finally became an obstacle for these gentlemen. It was necessary to force down wages and make rapid preparations for the new war. Little by little, brick by brick, the democratic edifice was dismantled: of course the constitution of the republic had wisely left this door open. Handing over power to fascism, the bourgeoisie dealt the final blow to a democracy no longer useful to it. But this also freed the German worker[2] from his illusions in a peaceful, democratic path to power and a "gradual evolution" toward socialism.

There is also the danger that the Stalinist party, which claims to be communist, will deprive the German working people of their revolution with the help of mass deception and G.P.U. terror,[3] much as the Social Democrats did 25 years ago. During the Spanish Civil War, the full extent of this danger was shown. But the danger should not be overestimated either. The capitalist governments' distrust obliges the Russian bureaucracy to unmask itself more and more in the eyes of the international proletariat. Moreover, it is precisely the German worker who is equipped against this malady. He can follow it to its roots. The misery of the Russian masses and the affluence of the bureaucrats teach him that after the failure of the German revolution and thus the European revolution, the victorious October Revolution remained isolated and was bound to (and did) collapse. On the other hand, this bureaucratic layer which came to power after Lenin's death constituted the center of the Third International, determining the leadership and policies of its member parties. The Russian bosses are no more willing or able to lead the masses into struggle than the S.P.D. or union bosses.

So it is wrong to think that the German workers have learned nothing since 1918. It is wrong to believe that the tragedy must be repeated. It is superficial to say that after ten years of fascist rule we must start all over again. In the years following the World War, the German proletarians enriched themselves with very bitter, but also very valuable, experiences. They experienced the decline of capitalism to a greater extent than the workers of almost any other country; they got to know the rottenness of bourgeois democracy well; they learned to distrust parties and to be careful in choosing their leaders.

All this recently won experience will only come to light in the struggle itself. When the rancor against the capitalist warmongers clears away the sludge of the fascists' obfuscating propaganda, it will not take the workers much time to learn and gain experience in struggle, since it is basically only a question of remembering, of passing knowledge from the older generation to the young. Gentlemen of London and Washington, Berlin and Moscow, be certain: although it is threatened by many dangers, the proletarian revolution is around the corner, even closer than you suspect in your nightmares.

The revolution is being prepared

The day of the revolution cannot be predicted. But its preparation begins long before it breaks out. When, after its quick victories over less well-armed and militarized peoples, the German army first met with serious resistance, the fascist attempt to deny class contradictions out of existence was also shown to be hollow. Fascism did succeed, using boundless terror, to banish class struggle from the surface for a certain time. But now it has reappeared. A process of decomposition began both at the front and in the rear. The rapture of victory was shattered, the enthusiasm for fighting disappeared, slow work and sabotage in the factories became more and more widespread, and only the bloodiest terror keeps the front and the economy afloat.

So far, only very few see the new goal. The smoke screen of the fascist propaganda has not yet been completely torn. The experiences of the German worker in uniform in Russia are still causing more confusion than clarity, more doubt than hope. Already, however, groups are forming everywhere to give answers. Old cells which survived the years of terror by keeping to themselves are again putting out feelers. New groups are being organized. New information is spreading, mouth to mouth and in print, in newspapers and leaflets. On the first day of open struggle, the best of these groups will unite to form the new revolutionary Communist Party.

"Worker and Soldier" places itself in this process of destroying fascist rule and all bourgeois rule, undermining the capitalist war front, re-establishing the proletarian class front and preparing the communist revolution. This defines all its tasks.

Peace! Freedom! Bread!

ON THE DISSOLUTION OF THE THIRD INTERNATIONAL

The Stalin-Bureaucrats have dissolved the Comintern. Beware, declares the Axis propaganda, only a maneuver, a disguise, playing dead. Hurrah, the Anglo-Saxon imperialist press cheers, our allies are not communists, they are pure Russian patriots. Yes, it's just a maneuver, the communist worker says to reassure himself, if he stuck with the Third International despite all the defeats; they are tricking the capitalist enemies, folding up the flag only to unfurl it again in the right moment. Maneuvers, he contemplates, are possible and even necessary against the class enemy. But he starts to have doubts: Is the dissolution of the International really just a subterfuge against the class enemy, or might it be a maneuver against the workers of the world?

Can the dissolution of the International be a maneuver of proletarian class struggle? "The importance of the struggle for the dictatorship of the proletariat requires a single, close-knit, international organization of all Communists who agree with this platform."[4] This is what the resolution which founded the Third International says. Whoever dissolves this organization, even if he only "appeared" to do so, even if only to confuse the enemy, is also confusing the workers about their task, namely the struggle for the dictatorship of the proletariat. Today when millions of oppressed people hope that the end of the second imperialist war will bring the end of all oppression and thus of all wars, today when society is facing violent revolutionary struggles, the dissolution of the International can only serve to paralyze the fighting strength of the proletarians, to discourage them and sow confusion in their ranks. No, such a maneuver is not directed against the class enemy – it is deception of working people and above all of the International's followers. This step is a clear departure from communist revolution.

It is not the first step of this kind made by the Russian bureaucrats. To only mention the most recent and the worst: In Spain, the proletarians' struggle against fascism and for the establishment of a council state is declared to be a "national liberation struggle." The councils are strangled, the revolutionary workers are terrorized with the help of the G.P.U. and thus the backbone of the resistance to Franco is broken. In France in June 1936, they put the brakes on the strike wave and force the nascent revolutionary movement into the narrow limits of the Popular Front fraud. In Germany, they promote a Popular Front "including the Stahlhelm"[5] with the objective of a "national people's government."

The dissolution of the proletarian front just before the rise of the new revolutionary wave is not simply a declaration of abandoning or rejection of the revolution. It is above all a declaration of war against the coming proletarian uprising. The surviving national organizations [of the Comintern] will have the task of suffocating any proletarian revolutionary struggle, following the Spanish model. The communist revolution is international, but it is to be strangled at a national level.

None of this will surprise the German proletarians. In the East, they see with their own eyes that the Russia of the Stalin bureaucracy has replaced Lenin's Russia of workers, peasants, and their soviets. Every bureaucracy has always been characterized by the deepest mistrust of the revolutionary potential of the masses. These bureaucrats have always considered themselves extremely clever and terribly "realistic." A thousand tanks, says Roosevelt, will only be sent if you dissolve the International. A thousand tanks and Roosevelt's trust, the bureaucrats say, are worth more than tomorrow's revolution and the masses' trust.

But in our time there is no realpolitik besides revolutionary politics. By turning away from the revolution, by betraying it and selling it out to Anglo-American capital, by their chauvinist agitation and cruel treatment of their prisoners, the bureaucrats only embitter the German soldier, obscuring the revolutionary solution for him and throwing him defenseless back into the arms of the Göbbels propaganda, thus prolonging the war. One German worker, upon receiving revolutionary material from a comrade, said: If these writings were distributed throughout Germany for only a few days, the war would be over and the revolution would be here. This worker had a more "realistic" political outlook than all the Russian bureaucrats have ever shown in the 25 years of their corrupt rule.

The German press, which presents the predatory war of capitalists like Krupp, Klöckner, Röchling, and Borsig[6] as a crusade against "Bolshevik chaos," must of course do all in its power to spread the fairy tale of this "maneuver." In this sense it also claims that the dissolved Third International will simply turn into the Fourth. The first fairy tale is basically flattery of the Stalinist bureaucracy – the second is an insult against the tool of the coming revolution. The Fourth International is in fact a formation, but as a rallying point for truly revolutionary communists. The work of Marx and Engels, Lenin and Trotsky, Liebknecht and Luxemburg should be continued. The new organization is being formed precisely in struggle against the betrayal by Stalin and his parties, not as some new edition of the Comintern. It represents a continuation of the Third International only insofar as it will fight to accomplish the goal set by Lenin's Comintern – long since betrayed by Stalin – in the coming revolutionary struggles: building a "single, close-knit, international organization to struggle for the dictatorship of the proletariat."

Revolutionary communists welcome the dissolution of the Comintern. Initially it will lead to discouragement and confusion in the proletarian ranks. However, against the will of the Stalin clique, it will ultimately facilitate the struggle for the proletarian objective of the coming revolution. Before the eyes of all proletarians it will place a seal on the betrayal by the Russian bosses and their Comintern. Ultimately it must convince all working people of the need to build a new revolutionary International.

––––––

Comrades!

You want to fight for the proletarian revolution. You are convinced of the need for a new revolutionary communist party. You want to win over your colleagues in the factory, your fellow soldiers at the front or in the barracks. You don't always succeed. Some are still Stalinists, others even hope for a resurrection of the S.P.D., a third wants to see the "good times" from before 33 again, and a fourth doesn't want to hear anything about politics. But you cannot let this prevent you from standing together with all of them when there are resistance actions against a factory manager, a tyrannical foreman, an officer who is mistreating people or against new reprisals by the Nazi clique. On the contrary. You, as revolutionary communists, <u>must be the first</u>! to distinguish yourselves with courage, energy, and caution. Many who you cannot win over today, even with the best arguments, can be electrified by your stance. Many will only find the courage to join us in the struggle itself.

––––––

July 19, 1936.

On that day seven years ago, General Franco attacked the Spanish republican government. With unparalleled vigor, the Spanish proletariat rose up, smashing the generals' uprising in Madrid and Barcelona. The republican government, unable to stop the reactionary putsch, was forced to retreat in the face of the revolutionary determination of the working masses. In Barcelona, the old Catalan government was replaced with the Central Committee of Militias, which exercised de facto governmental power. All political parties were represented in it. The Militia Committee was the Spanish form of the soviets. In Catalonia, Aragon, Valencia, and Malaga the movement went way beyond the limits of the bourgeois republic: expropriation measures, collectivization of landed estates, distribution of basic goods by workers' and peasants' cooperatives. The old Catalan government was a shadow of its former self. In these provinces, the workers and peasants held power in practice.

Not so in Madrid. From the outset, the Popular Front government tried to strip the mass movement of its revolutionary character. Expropriation measures against the bourgeoisie were taken only where unavoidable. A fierce struggle was launched against the workers' and peasants' committees. The main representatives of this tendency were the republicans, the right-wing socialists and the communists. A decision had to be made between these two poles: reformist Madrid and revolutionary Barcelona.

The international situation was marked by the weakness of the proletariat. There was a powerful movement of factory occupations in France. But here too, the mass movement collapsed, leading to a simple Popular Front government. Together, communists and social democrats put the brakes on the movement, robbing it of its political edge. The Great Powers each took a position. The so-called "democratic powers" were for non-intervention, even though it was a struggle against the uprising of reactionary generals. The fascist powers sent aid to Franco from day one. The Soviet Union initially took part in the farce of non-intervention, then withdrew to support the bourgeois republic. Certainly not the revolutionary mass movement. All the arms shipments from the U.S.S.R. to Spain had one sole aim: preventing the workers' revolution and consolidating the bourgeois republic. Weapons were only delivered to organizations that loyally adhered to this line.

In just the second month of the war, the Russians demanded the dissolution of the Central Militia Committee in Barcelona and the restoration of the old bourgeois government. After some weak resistance, the anarchists gave in. The workers', peasants', and militia committees were deprived of their authority and were gradually dissolved. The G.P.U. organized the persecution and suppression of the revolutionary workers' organizations.

The will of the proletarian masses rose up against this anti-proletarian policy one more time in Catalonia, Aragon, and Valencia in 1937 in May. In a three-day uprising, the masses conquered the streets and paralyzed the communist and republican formations. Unfortunately, there was no proletarian party to direct the masses to their goal. The betrayal of the anarchist leaders decapitated the movement and the uprising ran out of steam. The defeat of the revolutionary movement broke the back of the struggle against Franco. The fascist uprising could not be crushed on the basis of defending the bourgeois republic.

How can the communists' position be explained?

There is only one decisive reason: the Russian bureaucracy knows only one political principle: staying in power and remaining at the feeding trough. Every revolutionary mass movement threatens the bureaucracy's position of power. Therefore every revolutionary movement is its mortal enemy. No revolution! No difficulties with the imperialist Great Powers! The Russian bureaucracy is the incarnation of counter-revolution. It is not about Stalin. The bureaucracy is a social layer, a new generation that is educated in spotless nationalism, a disgusting sense of entitlement and parasitism. The bureaucracy would sacrifice everything to remain in power, including the social and political gains of the October Revolution.

The Spanish example shows: A revolution cannot succeed without a revolutionary party. It was missing in Spain and the revolution perished. Moreover: Any future one will have as its enemy not only the local bourgeoisie but also the Russian bureaucracy. We must take both these lessons into account in the coming German and European revolutions.

———

THE BELGIAN WORKING CLASS IN THE WAR

The Belgian workers, the majority of whom sensed that the war was being waged solely in the interests of the big capitalists, entered the fight extremely reluctantly. That was one of the main reasons for the rapid defeat, which prevented many casualties among the Belgian population. However, the workers' movement suffered a heavy blow after the German victory. A wave of nationalism and enthusiasm for the R.A.F. swept over the country, penetrating far into circles of the working-class. The main reason for this was the deterioration of living standards caused by the loss of imports and the export of food and coal to Germany. One of the first German decrees fixed wages, shifting the misery onto the working class.

The workers and their families tried to eke out a meager living with Sunday trips to the countryside where food had not become so expensive. Those unable to do so went to Germany "voluntarily." Despite the poverty of the working class, or more correctly because of it, the Belgian and German industrialists producing arms did excellent business. Prices rose, but wages remained fixed. Thus the Belgian proletarians made their first acquaintance with national socialism.

During the winter of 1942, the German authorities began mass deportations of workers to Germany. A protest strike broke out in a large factory of about 10000 workers in Liege. After a three-day strike, the authorities postponed the deportation of the workers in big industry until February 1943. Now, especially in the province of Liege, there was a feverish regeneration of the workers' organizations to resist the deportations. New class-conscious trade unions were formed to replace the old destroyed ones. For the first time, the still weak revolutionary communist party gained a foothold among the workers in heavy industry.

When the defensive strike against the deportations broke out at the end of February – 30000 workers went on strike in the province of Liege alone – the following interesting spectacle was immediately observed: the capitalist directors helped the German authorities break the strike. In this way, the workers saw that all the talk of a national front was just a bluff as soon as the owners' profits were threatened and the excellent business was to be interrupted for even a few days.

The workers feared that in the event of riots or demonstrations the German soldiers, deceived by the military administration, would open fire on the population. A leaflet circulated among the workers of heavy industry calling for fraternization with the German workers in field-gray [uniforms] who wanted to return to their homes just as much as the Belgian worker wanted to stay with his family. Although there were no struggles and the fraternization did not materialize, the leaflet had a profound impact on the workers. They realized who the real enemy was and where their true ally was to be found. The first step toward struggle had replaced the artificial national front with the class front of the Belgian and German workers against the Belgian and German capitalists and their military satellites.

The struggle ended after three days. It proved that the new organization was still too weak and too inexperienced to hold the masses together against the reprisals of the German oppression machine. These struggles are basically the preparation for the coming revolutionary period. The defeat of the workers can therefore only discourage them for a short time. They recognized their mistakes and resolved to put their experience to use in the next struggle. The organizing continues. In some large factories there have even been new strikes to prevent further deterioration of the standard of living.

Workers, soldiers!

Many foreign workers, misled by the bourgeoisie's inflammatory propaganda, believe that you are all fascists. They believe that you wanted the war. They reproach you for not having thrown down your guns, as they did. They do not see the system of lies, terror, and espionage that forced you into the fight. Talk to them wherever you can! Explain your situation to them! Tell them that you also want nothing more than the end of this war. Tell them that you are preparing for this outcome and for the common proletarian reckoning with the class enemy! In doing so today, you secure the proletarian revolution of tomorrow. In doing so, you contribute to its transformation into the European revolution. In doing so, you have a better and more effective foreign policy than any bourgeois minister!

DO YOU REMEMBER:

1) that in July 1917 a powerful workers' demonstration took place in Petrograd? At the time, the Bolshevik Party under Lenin's leadership was a revolutionary party. The Bolsheviks recognized that the countryside and the front were not yet ripe for the conquest of power by the proletariat and that Petrograd and Moscow had hurried too far ahead. That is why they tried to prevent the action. This proved to be a mistake because the leadership of the masses threatened to fall into the hands of anarchists and provocateurs. They recognized their error and soon corrected it. The party now tried to keep the movement in the limits of an armed but peaceful demonstration, which was partially accomplished. Thanks to its level-headed attitude, after the collapse of the action the party won the confidence of the best proletarian militants. Nevertheless, a massive smear campaign began. The Bolsheviks were slandered as agents of Ludendorff. Lenin and Zinoviev were forced into hiding. Trotsky, Lunacharsky, and others were thrown into prison. However, three months later, they seized power and handed it over to the second congress of the Russian councils.

2) that in July 1932 the Papen government deposed the Social Democratic ministers in Prussia, Braun and Severing? The S.P.D. bosses held back the workers. The Reich government had acted in a perfectly "legal" fashion. Besides, there would soon be elections. A ballot paper instead of a gun. – The K.P.D. called a general strike. But no one listened. Why? Because just a year earlier it had called on workers to vote with the Nazis in a referendum against these same Prussian ministers. Because its policy of building its own union (R.G.O.)[7] had isolated it from the workers in the factories. Because the theory of social fascism repelled the Social Democratic workers who wanted to fight. That was how it prepared the worst of all defeats, a defeat without a fight.

––––––

Fed up with these big mouths again.

"From now on, dear *Volksgenossen* [national comrades], rations will only increase. The surplus in the Ukraine which this year has already

... etc. etc." Thus spoke the party's propaganda heroes, Hitler, Göring, and Göbbels, last winter. Everything depended on the front holding, so that the war and the war profits would last for a long time. That is what the gentlemen of heavy industry, Drupp, Siemens, and Röchling and others, wanted.

Promising and keeping a promise are two different things. Now they have cut the meat ration by 100g a week. Of course without forgetting lame excuses. The proletarians are tightening their belts and clenching the fists they will use, when the time is right, to shut up these big mouths.

———

PEACE! FREEDOM! BREAD!

PEACE, total peace, no more war, can only be achieved by proletarian revolution.

FREEDOM, for all the exploited is possible only in the socialist council republic.

BREAD, for all, elimination of economic crises, can only be accomplished by the expropriation of capital and the establishment of a socialist planned economy.

Notes

1. In German, the term *das Kapital* can refer to the entirety of the capitalist class and its capital (a synecdoche). "Capital" in this sense is less common in English, but is used here.
2. The term "the German soldier" or "the German worker" is similarly used to refer to all members of these groups.
3. The State Political Directorate (GPU) or Joint State Political Directorate (OGPU) was the secret police of the Soviet Union until 1934. Then it was integrated into the People's Commissariat for Internal Affairs (NKVD), but the old name was still widely used.
4. "Proposal to Constitute the Third International," Alix Holt and Barbara Holland, eds., *Theses, Resolutions and Manifestos of the First Four Congress of the Third International* (London: Ink Links, 1980), 20.
5. The *Stahlhelm* or "Steel Helmet" was a right-wing German paramilitary organization that existed from 1918 to 1935 as the armed wing of the

German National People's Party (DNVP). It was largely merged into the Nazis' SA in 1933 and its leader served as Hitler's Minister of Labor from 1933–45.

6. Gustav Krupp (1870–1950), Peter Klöckner (1863–1940), Hermann Röchling (1872–1955), and Ernst Borsig (1869–1933) were all German big industrialists who supported the Nazis.

7. The Revolutionary Trade Union Opposition (RGO) was a "red" trade union founded by the Communist Party of Germany in 1930.

The German Revolution is the World Revolution.
K. Liebknecht

WORKER and SOLDIER

Organ for proletarian-revolutionary unification – fourth International
No. 2
August 1943

ON BEHALF OF WORLD CAPITAL

The beginning of the workers' revolution in Germany is approaching. The workers of Italy are already on the move; in the Balkans, in Portugal and Spain military rule and fascist dictatorships are crumbling. How much time can be left until the German worker and soldier will break the chains of fascism and the great struggle will begin throughout Europe, between the exploited and the exploiters?

It is high time for the Anglo-American capitalists to prepare for the salvation of German and European capital. No matter how fervently and ferociously the brothers of high finance wage war against each other with the blood of the workers, they will all the more fervently and fraternally help each other when the sacred right to capitalist property and capitalist exploitation is in question. These gentleman know how contagious workers' revolutions can be, now more than ever.

Arms alone will not be enough to fight against the European revolution. The people carrying the weapons on the Anglo-Saxon side are themselves workers and peasants. They could still be mobilized against a fascist Germany. Will they let themselves be misled into fighting against a proletarian Europe? Didn't [the bourgeoisie] already have quite unpleasant experiences in 1918–19 when it tried to strangle the victorious October Revolution of workers and peasants in Russia? The mutiny of the French fleet in the Black Sea and the strikes by English dockers who were supposed to ship arms to Russia may well have left more traces in the memory of the big capitalists than in the consciousness of the world's working class.

And has much changed in the 25 years since then? The English working class has radicalized. In 1926 the miners, betrayed by the union bureaucrats, went on strike for a whole year. During the capitalist crisis, the American paradise was transformed into hell with 13 million unemployed workers. Even during the war we hear of strikes by miners, transport workers, and armaments workers in England or a strike of 600000 mineworkers in America. Will the English and American workers want to fight if the revolutionary proletarians of Europe educate them about their real interests and tasks and fraternize with them? This is not as simple as Messrs. Churchill and Roosevelt present it. They know that perfectly well themselves, which is why they do not want to fight the revolutionary masses of Europe, above all those of Germany, with tanks and machine guns alone, but with a much more effective weapon: a poisonous injection.

This poisonous injection was used by the bourgeoisie in Germany in 1918 to restrain the working class in its revolutionary struggle. The bosses of Social Democracy disoriented the proletarians with lies and false promises, inciting one part of the class against another and gradually destroying the gains of the revolution. But the bosses of Social Democracy have been used up. In 1933, after the transfer of power to Hitler, their laughable nature was on full display for the German workers. This time around, world capital needs another henchman to inject poison into the blood of the workers of Germany and all Europe: the bureaucracy in Moscow, which has put its boot on the neck of the victorious but isolated October Revolution, is to complete this task. Despite all the little disputes in the haggling about borders, it was in the interests of the finance capital of the world that the Russian bureaucracy sent the latest dose of poison to the address of the German revolution.

AN APPEAL FROM MOSCOW

The Moscow radio station has announced the formation of a "National Committee for a Free Germany." This committee is composed of an émigré poet as president, captured generals, etc. The ex-communist poet and the ex-fascist generals have published a manifesto, with 5 points of particular interest for German workers.

1) They claim that the terrible hardship that has befallen the working people of Germany is the work of one man, Hitler.

2) All followers of Hitler who renounce him in time will be pardoned.

3) The German soldiers on the front should march on Berlin and overthrow Hitler, <u>under the leadership of their generals</u>.

4) A "strong," "independent," and "national" government is to be established.

5) Legally acquired property will be guaranteed.

GERMAN WORKERS AND SOLDIERS!

Remember: What happened in 1918? The Kaiser fled and the generals remained. A fake democratic facade was erected in the foreground. The same thing now! In the interests of big capital, Moscow proposes that you repeat the tragedy of 1918. With one small difference: This time around the democratic spectacle will be smaller. What will the German workers, the German toilers do? They will send Moscow's dose of poison, neatly packed, back to Stalin with a note: no longer effective this time!

For their part, they will make five counterproposals:

1) When the accounts are settled, Hitler will not be neglected. But we will not forget that he and his clique were acting in the service of big capital. The big industrial barons and the bankers in Germany wanted and waged this war just as much as the first one, and they will provoke a third war if we do not put a complete stop to their machinations.

2) If Göring or some other Nazi boss or Gestapo executioner soils his pants today and breaks from his beloved Führer, it will be of little use to him.

3) We will find our way home, without our generals. We entrusted them with this task in 1918. <u>That is why they could march us away from home again in 1939</u>. On the first day of the revolution, we will abolish all officers and all ranks. We will elect soldiers' councils which will take command and supervise the specialists.

4) We do not want an "independent," "national" government! This government would not be independent of either the victorious capitalists or our own. This means it would be: independent of the workers! On the contrary, we want <u>a government of the working people themselves</u>. The best way to achieve this is the council system. This time we will not let the councils be taken from us with swindles like in 1918.

5) The petty grafters and the big war profiteers of big industry have made their profits in a "legal" fashion and acquired their giant fortunes more or less "lawfully." That is because they made the laws themselves. The workers will nevertheless confiscate their businesses and furthermore create laws that oblige everyone to work and prohibit all exploitation.

———

PEACE! FREEDOM! BREAD!

———

WE *LANDSER* [SOLDIERS] AND THE ITALIAN EVENTS

The sparse coverage of the events in Italy by the Nazi press has been noted by the German soldier with concern and anger. But fellow soldiers who return from Italy and report on the events there inform him that he is not allowed to know anything about the miserable bankruptcy of the fascists, so that the parallels which jump to mind do not shed light on the conditions in his own country.

Fascism has gone bankrupt because of its internal falsehood and its totally corrupt system of party chieftains which had no objective other than to exploit the Italian people and above all the Italian workers.

Tens of thousands of fascist militiamen threw down their weapons and defected when the English and Americans landed. Is this the fascists' strength that Mussolini so often boastfully proclaimed? The German soldier in Sicily had to suffer and bleed after being sent there by the Nazis and betrayed by the fascists. But what actually happened in Italy? Can the Italian worker be held responsible for this? As the lamentable failure of the fascist "art of the state" and the stinking corruption of a bloodsucking party bureaucracy became ever more obvious, a reaction against this activity grew among the Italian workers. As the people's reluctance became more apparent, finally resulting in strikes as its clearest and most determined expression, the army and the king acted to preempt the Italian revolution and save what they could at the last minute. The strikes were bloodily suppressed and a state of emergency was declared. But in the long run, these measures can only delay and no longer prevent the victory of a just cause, the victory of the working class over fascism and imperialism of all stripes.

Knowing what happened in Italy and the speed at which the phantom of Mussolini dissolved, it is easy to understand the embarrassed restraint of the Nazi press when reporting on Italy. The German soldier should not be allowed to draw parallels. He must be made stupid by the propaganda hammered into his head every day so he does not start thinking. In Berlin they know how dangerous such thoughts can and will become for the Nazis' high party apparatus. It is not the Italian people who are to blame if you speak about a disloyal ally, but fascism is. Think about that when you talk about what is yet to come. The whole world is today the victim of the fascists' madness for power and the capitalists' greed for profit. Stalin, who betrayed the proletarian revolution, has become the henchman of that imperialist-capitalist clique.

The current war, in its senseless awfulness, will prepare the ground for the coming revolution of the workers of all countries. The Fourth International will lead it to victory.

A guy from the infantry

Note of the editorial board: We sign the comrade's letter with both hands. We would go even further: There can be no talk of guilt of the Italian workers, only of their achievements. If in this war, which is waged not in the interest of the workers but in the interests of capital, the proletarians finally rise up somewhere, be it in England, America or Germany, Russia or Italy, there can be no talk of betrayal.

We must not speak about the guilt of the Italian workers but rather about the weakness of the German workers who are still letting themselves be driven to the slaughterhouse in the name of Hitler and in the interests of Krupp and Borsig.

———

All of you
who are in contact with our comrades, write to "Worker and Soldier" about your opinions and experiences!!!!!!
It is your newspaper!

———

TALK OF POLITICS FORBIDDEN!!

The closer the war gets to its end, the quieter the people at the top become, Adolf, Hermann, Joseph and Co. The people at the bottom, the workers and soldiers, raise their voice and become louder and easier to hear. Everywhere people are discussing what should happen tomorrow when the war is over. Even the high authorities, who according to Göbbels know everything, have noticed this. Now they are trying to intervene with the old familiar means. Soldiers in different units have been forbidden from talking about politics. But the old magic is not working any more. They continue to talk about politics vehemently, now more than ever. This murmuring, this whispering is the distant roar of the approaching revolution.

PEACE! FREEDOM! BREAD!

COUNCIL GERMANY[1]
HOW WE WANT IT AND HOW WE DO NOT WANT IT

The degeneration of the Russian Revolution of 1917 resulted from many particularities of Russia's situation. A backward agricultural country, a politically weak bourgeoisie with shallow roots in society, a Bolshevik Party that combined an audacious will and a firm resolve facilitated the workers' conquest of power. After the conquest of power, these circumstances proved to be obstacles. The leaden weight of the vast, ignorant peasant masses made the industrialization and administration of the country difficult. The failure of the European revolution, particularly the German revolution, added to the difficulties. The Bolshevik Party disintegrated in internal struggles. It gave birth to a bureaucracy which ruled over the masses as the Tsar's cabal used to. What is happening in Russia today – the functioning of a bureaucracy which by tradition still occasionally uses Bolshevik formulas – has nothing in common with socialism.

The conditions of the German revolution and the construction of a socialist society in Europe are different than in Russia. Below we show how we picture this construction in Germany:

WE WANT the real dictatorship of the proletariat, which means a democracy of all working people. The basis for workers' democracy will be the comprehensive organization of councils. (Workers, salaried employees, small farmers.) The council organization is the highest authority. As the most conscious part of the class, the party fulfills its task within the framework of the councils.

WE DO NOT WANT the councils to be the powerless tool of a party which is itself the mindless instrument of a clique. We reject the rule of a party and state bureaucracy in place of the rule of the working class.

WE WANT the broadest democracy for the workers, that is: no coercion regarding conscience or religion, freedom of the press, freedom of speech, unlimited right of assembly and association for all parties that are based on the council system.

WE DO NOT WANT the tyranny of a party. We reject the repression of workers' parties that are for a workers' government via councils.

WE WANT people's tribunals established by the working people which deliberate and pass judgment publicly.

WE DO NOT WANT a G.P.U. that arbitrarily arrests, deports, and shoots people while avoiding public attention. We do not want a legal system which does not recognize rights but only brute force.

WE WANT the control of all leading authorities by the working people themselves. Election and recall at any time.

WE DO NOT WANT the arbitrary rule a bureaucracy that suppresses every free initiative by the workers.

WE WANT the administration and distribution of production by the workers themselves. The organs of the workers' state (councils), in collaboration with trade unions and cooperatives, will draw up and implement the program for production and distribution.

WE DO NOT WANT the dictatorial management of production and distribution by a caste of bureaucrats who pocket whatever they please. But this is what exists in Russia.

———

HAMBURG AND NOW BERLIN TOO

In the last war there were still fronts. In this one the rear also became a front. Especially the proletarians in Hamburg have had to learn this bitter lesson. While the English chemical trust receives a blessing of millions of pounds, the English air fleet is dropping millions of kilograms of explosives on the German workers and their families. But we must not fool ourselves. Our own exploiters and warmongering hyenas are not one bit better. If the German war machine had been able to do so it would have prepared the same fate for the working people in London. If we want to stop the repetition of such atrocities forever we must march hand in hand with the London proletarians against the common enemy, German and English capital. We must begin now. Down with the Nazi bosses! Stop the war! Get rid of capitalism!

———

ONE LESS – BUT ONLY ONE

According to a comrade's report, the mayor of Wuppertal has been removed. When the alarm sounded, the fellow drove to the countryside in the evening and returned to the rubble in the morning very drunk. The Nazi clique sacrificed him. But how many of those who disappear in the evening are clever enough and drive back to town unseen? One of them had to go, but how many remain? Time to chase the whole Nazi gang to hell.

—————

DO YOU REMEMBER:

1) that in the first days of August 1914 the first imperialist world war began? On our side they said: fight the Tsar. On the other: fight the Kaiser. In reality both sides were interested in capitalist war profits, capitalist markets and redivision of colonial territories among imperialist slave-owners. This time only the slogans have changed. The content and the real aims of the war are exactly the same again. Colonial profits, not democracy or national socialism. Lenin said back then: either the proletarian revolution will triumph or there will be another, even more terrible war. The words of Lenin are true now as then.

2) that the Weimar Constitution was completed in August 1919 as the masterpiece of the National Assembly? In this Constitution of professors, lawyers, and party bosses etc. there was much talk of freedom. But it also included the infamous Article 48 which made all these fine freedoms subject to the mood of the Reich President, i.e. of capital. The emergency decrees of 1930 were thus prepared in 1919. Hindenburg appointed Hitler as Chancellor constitutionally. But even the best constitution could not have prevented that. The decisive question is who holds power, capital or the workers. In 1919 the Freikorps were able to nip the nascent proletarian revolution in the bud. So capital and its servants made the constitution. In 1943/44 it must be the councils, the revolutionary organs of workers and soldiers, which draw up a new constitution under the protection of red workers' guards.

Note

1. The German revolution of 1918–23 was defined by workers' and soldiers' councils, which in German are called *Räte*. In Russian, these are called

"soviets." The German word for the councils in Russia is *Sowjets*. Under Stalinization in the early 1930s, the Communist Party of Germany started to call for a *Sowjet-Deutschland*, implying a particularly close link to the Soviet Union. But before that, Communists always used the more local term *Räte-Deutschland*. Accordingly, we have used the term "Council Germany" instead of "Soviet Germany."

The German Revolution is the World Revolution.
K. Liebknecht

WORKER AND SOLDIER

Organ for proletarian-revolutionary unification – fourth International
No. 3
September 1943

WE WANT DEFEAT

We want the defeat of our capitalist class in this war. Let all the knights of industry and the bank barons, all the Nazi bosses and the generals, and all those who are still blinded and deceived by them clamor against the "betrayal of the fatherland" and shout "agents of the enemy." We will hold firm. We want the defeat of our capitalists; we prefer that to their victory.

The imperialist war is not a war for the little people. It is a war for big capital. On both sides of the fronts. After the last war there was talk of victorious peoples and defeated peoples. This was a lie. THE VICTORS WERE THE CAPITALISTS OF ALL COUNTRIES. THE DEFEATED WERE THE WORLD WORKING CLASS.

In the so-called defeated countries – we German proletarians know this best – the lords of industry used inflation to pass the costs of war and reconstruction on to the workers and the middle classes. Even in the worst moments, the big capitalists and the cleverest speculators were able to enrich themselves. On the other side, in the victorious countries, the working class had to fight hard to regain a tolerable standard of living.

But the imperialist victory meant not only the economic but also the political defeat of the workers. The capitalist class (and every ruling class) has always utilized its military victories to put new chains on the oppressed class. Let us briefly recall: In the 2 years of victories over the European population, did the national socialist state loosen our shackles even a millimeter? Were we allowed to say freely what we thought and [...]? Haven't the brothers of the Gestapo become even more self-assured and insolent?

Let us read what Göbbels [...] in a rare flash of honesty: "It must therefore be the case that the external freedom of a nation is paid for with a certain degree of internal compulsion" (Das Reich, August 29, 1943). Is that not clear enough? External freedom, that is to say the oppression of the French, Poles, Russians, Negroes, and Indians, is paid for with a "certain degree of internal compulsion," which as we all know means the Gestapo and the Nazi whip for the German worker.

Even if Germany had won the war and German capital had filled its huge pockets with the profits from the exploitation of hundreds of millions of colonial slaves, there would still have been oppression and exploitation for the German worker [...] Certainly, some [...] would have advanced into a "better" position as slave overseers or police henchmen for our capitalist masters. It was for this purpose that the Nazis, certain of victory, created the theory of the supreme German race.

Class-conscious proletarians want nothing to do with that. They struggle for the emancipation of the colonial slaves and for the abolition of all oppression, not for a comfortable position as a whip-holder for the lords of industry. "A people that oppresses others cannot be free," said Marx. He who fights for colonial conquests is, at the end of the day, fighting for his own oppression. The final and ironclad conclusion of this obliges us to say boldly and clearly: We do not want the victory of our capital in the imperialist war of plunder.

Moreover. We do not only damn the victory of our own robbers against the brigands on the other side. We want their defeat. Defeat in revolutionary[1] wars led to the first uprisings of the revolutionary class: 1871 in France, 1905 and 1917 in Russia, 1918 in Germany. Therefore Lenin coined the principle for workers of all countries: "In a reactionary war, the revolutionary class must wish for the defeat of its own government."

Every prolongation of the imperialist war means further sacrifices, of strength and health, of property and life, above all for the working class. That is why we want the defeat of our government as soon as possible. But the means that can lead to defeat and a rapid end to the imperialist war are not desertion, sabotage, or terror. Only the means of the proletarian class struggle can lead to victory. In the Russian

Revolution of 1917 one soldier said, "Sticking the bayonet in the ground is not yet peace." To hasten the end of the war we must build proletarian revolutionary organizations everywhere.

Such organizations can spread the first local outburst of anger by the working masses against oppression by big capital and the Nazi clique and against their senseless war, leading to an abrupt collapse of the system. It is for this reason, among others, that fascism suppressed every independent working-class organization, so it could wage war for as long as possible and as undisturbedly as possible. So let us be clear about the fact that every new local group and every new cell we create is a part of the work for peace. And not only for the end of this war, but for the elimination of all wars. Because the proletarian revolutionary party fights first and foremost to push the revolution forward to the end, until the capitalist system is replaced by socialism.

STOP THE WAR! DOWN WITH THE NAZI TYRANNY! FOR A COUNCIL STATE!

To achieve this we fight for the defeat of our own capitalism. We revolutionaries know that this will provoke much hatred and slander. Was Lenin not accused of being an agent of Ludendorff? Did the lying bourgeois press not assail Liebknecht and other honest fighters of the proletarian revolution with the slander that they had been bribed by the enemy? Aware that the great truth of the revolutionary class must break through all the petty lies of reaction, we raise the flag of the defeat of our capitalism, the flag of the working class.

PEACE! – FREEDOM! – BREAD!

———

FOUR YEARS OF WORLD WAR.

1. The military balance sheet

First and second year of the war: Victory after victory across Europe. <u>Clear superiority of the Axis</u>.

Third year: First setback in the East. Retreat in places during the severe winter. But in summer a final significant offensive. In Africa, after the advantage shifts back and forth, a German advance as far as the Pyramids. Balanced forces.

Fourth year: Enormous retreat in the East. Loss of North Africa, Sicily, Italy. Bombardment of the North German cities. With the advance of the Anglo-Americans, threats to the cities of South Germany are also to be expected. Clear superiority of the Axis' opponents.

The explanation of this development: Since 1933, all production, all economics, all politics, and all life in Germany was systematically directed toward war. Hence the great advantage.

The enemy in the imperialist war had much larger reserves at its disposal. The enormous American industry, the raw materials from the greater part of the world, the extent of the huge Russian empire.

What does this mean for the future? That the war is definitively lost. The enemy mobilizes more and more of its reserves. Ours are dwindling. Mr. Göbbels hopes (i.e. he pretends to) for a Russian collapse. It is true that there is a food shortage for the Russians. But the Americans send them enough for them to hold out. The Russians are constantly on the advance. The third winter will undoubtedly bring them significant territorial gains and threaten the East of Germany.

The only ones in favor of prolonging the war are those who profit from it, big capital and its servants in politics and the military, the Nazis and the generals.

2. The balance sheet of the workers

Seventy-hour week. Paper money and empty slogans as wages. Deterioration of the food situation, lack of clothes and the most necessary household items. Destroyed homes, housing shortage. Families torn apart, family happiness destroyed forever. Limbs mutilated, shot up, frozen. People crippled, incurably sick. Millions of dead, burned, shot, stabbed, suffocated, and drowned. Men, women, and children. Which family has not yet suffered any losses?

3. The balance sheet of big capital

Right on the first of September, the fourth anniversary of the beginning of the war, the *Berliner Börsenzeitung*[2] published figures on German capital stock. Here we add the corresponding figures for 1939.

In billions of marks	1939	1941	1942
Total capital stock	20.29	24.9	29
Companies with more than 10 [?] million marks	7.97	11.2	14.1
As a percentage of total capital		39% 45%	48.5%

The bottom line is of particular interest for the working class. It shows that big capital has grown faster than small capital. In addition to newly built facilities, big capital has swallowed part of small and medium capital.

Capital is enriching itself with the blood and sweat of the workers [...] one thing is needed: a proletarian revolutionary final accounting [...]

PEACE! FREEDOM! BREAD!

THE REAL FACE OF THE WAR

"The Wehrmacht High Command reports."

"We were still about 50 km from Charkow [Kharkiv]. We pushed forward in the heaviest fighting. In the morning we received mail. This included a newspaper. We must have looked wide-eyed when we saw it announced the seizure of Charkow in bold letters. It was eight days later that we actually took Charkow."

"Fit for use at the front"

"My brother had lost several fingers to frostbite. He also had frost wounds on his feet. Which didn't stop the dogs from sending him out again. He stayed in the East......"

"From a letter from Hamburg"

"...the dead were piled up and burned with flamethrowers. I can only tell you: don't come back here. You won't recognize the city anymore..."

"Being blessed with children is a joy for the fatherland"

"We had to stay in the line of fire for fourteen days. Then we could rest again for eight days. Some of us stayed out there forever. Sch. and K. received news of the birth of their children just as they were supposed to return to the front. Midway they turned back. I never saw them again. They were shot immediately."

"The family is the foundation of the national socialist state"

"My two brothers have fallen, one in Russia, the other in Africa. During the last bombardment my wife and child died in Berlin. I knew nothing about the fate of my parents. When I asked the lieutenant for information he replied: We have more important things to do. – Now I have received news that father and mother are dead as well."

We reproduce one fellow soldier's outcry from a soldiers' newspaper of comrades from the Fourth International.

"You know, fellow soldiers, that Hamburg suffered the worst attack on 07/25/43. The murderous arsonist was over Hamburg not just once: no, five times. This is no longer a war. It is just murder and more murder. 280000 German women, children, and workers had to give their lives just because they are German.

I have lost everything. And for whom? Just because the capitalist dog, just because the capitalist dog[3] wants to live better and swim in his fat.

Dear fellow soldiers, we must put an end to this murder and tell ourselves that none of this makes sense. Promises were made to us which have not been kept to this day. Fellow soldiers, this can't be continued any further. So join us. Together we want to make a quick end to the war."

PEACE! FREEDOM! BREAD!

PEACE, total peace, no more war, can only be achieved by proletarian world revolution.

FREEDOM, for all the exploited is possible only in the socialist council republic.

BREAD, for all, elimination of economic crisis, can only be accomplished by the expropriation of capital and the establishment of a socialist planned economy.

Notes

1. Should read: reactionary.
2. A Berlin newspaper focusing on the stock market.
3. Repetition in the original.

[APRIL–MAY 1944]
PROLETARIANS OF ALL COUNTRIES, UNITE!

WORKER AND SOLDIER

ORGAN OF THE LEAGUE OF COMMUNIST-INTERNATIONAL-ISTS (GERMAN SECTION OF THE FOURTH INTERNATIONAL)

THE GERMAN REVOLUTION IS THE WORLD REVOLUTION!
(Karl Liebknecht)

FROM MAY 1, 1944: SET COURSE FOR THE REVOLUTION!

A fateful day for the German workers

In the First World War, the betrayal of the S.P.D. leadership left the German working class without a helm and a compass. The revolutionary word was suppressed by the state of emergency. It was a liberating act when Karl Liebknecht organized a demonstration at the Potsdamer Platz on May 1, 1916 with the participation of thousands of Berlin workers and called out to the workers, particularly the German workers: **This war is not our war.** It has to be transformed into a proletarian revolution. The main enemy is at home.[1] – Of course Liebknecht was thrown in jail by the capitalist state's guardians of the law. But the liberating word had been spoken.

The revolution arrived with the Kiel sailors' uprising, putting an end to the war. All of Germany was covered with a network of workers' and soldiers' councils. The bourgeois order shook to its foundations. But German capital was able to hold onto power, especially with the help of the social democratic bureaucrats. The councils were dissolved or transformed into the blunt instrument of works councils. Instead of peace, freedom, and bread, the German worker now received ballot papers, inflation, and the Reichswehr.

In the following period there were two May Day celebrations in Germany: that of the reformists, whom millions of workers still trusted despite their betrayal, and that of the young Communist Party, the German section of the Third International, whose task was to win the majority of the working class for the socialist revolution and lead it to power. The Third International naturally had its center of gravity in Russia, where the workers had taken power under the leadership of Lenin and Trotsky's Bolshevik Party. But the victorious revolution of the Russian workers' and peasants remained isolated due to the failure of the German revolution. This fact, exacerbated by the country's economic backwardness, inevitably led to the bureaucratization of the proletarian state and thus of the Bolshevik Party itself. Beginning with its center, the whole Third International ossified. Even its second-strongest party, the C.P. of Germany, became a branch of the Stalinist bureaucracy without any connection to the working masses.

The May Day celebration of 1929 made this clear. In line with its inner-Russian interests, the center in Moscow had decreed from its ivory tower[2] a new revolutionary period. This was a long ways from reality. To justify this leadership, revolutionary spectacles had to be staged artificially. May 1 was chosen for this. In many parts of Germany and especially in Berlin, the communist workers were called on to build barricades. The social democratic police chief Zorgiebe[3] used the good opportunity to throw his troops against the isolated communist workers. Despite their heroic defense, they were crushed. Their supporters were disheartened and the social democratic workers were indignant and appalled – that was the balance sheet of this mad adventure.

Bureaucrats never learn, not even from the bloodiest defeat of their followers. The errors of the Communist Party piled up. Confused by the theory of social fascism, the policy of splitting the unions and the tactic of the united front from below, the revolutionary proletariat was driven from defeat to defeat, up until the decisive one: the victory of the Nazi Party without a fight.

The Nazis made May 1, 1933 a national holiday. One more time – and this would be the last – the social democratic leaders and trade union bosses showed themselves in all their wretchedness. Attempting to buy mercy from their new master, these Judases called on their followers to participate in the Nazis' celebration. They did not receive the 30 shillings.

It was entirely in line with the Nazis' methods to keep May 1 as a holiday. They use slogans such as German socialism, "the honor of work," and "the common good before self-interest" etc. to mask the most barren exploitation and the most unrestricted rule of [...].[4] They place a shovel in the hands of the German worker and let him dig his own grave in piecework. Because bombs, tanks, and battleships were being produced. The capitalist state can only revive the economy by preparing for war. The war came.

The period of victories, which was due to Germany's head start in armaments, is over. It is not yet possible to say how many victims the second imperialist world war will claim, especially among the German workers. They have been driven to slaughter in the four corners of Europe, while wife and child, house and home were pulverized by bombs.

The war, which was lost from the outset due to the manifold superiority of American technology, will not last ten or fifteen years, as German, British, and American capital dreamed, and for this the workers of the world are indebted to the Russian workers who, despite the oppressive burden of bureaucratic parasitic rule, repelled the capitalist attack against the first proletarian state and thus saved the great gain of the October revolution, the planned economy.

We must rebuild the class front!

Today, in May 1944, the vast majority of the European population is still under the German jackboot. But the developments both at home and abroad show that the end is near. It may come from one day to the next. **But that does not mean that it will come by itself.** The Nazi clique and its capitalist backers are determined to hold out to the last German worker. Overthrowing the reign of terror, ending the war – like in 1918, this can only be achieved by the workers themselves. **Peace can only be won through revolution. But which peace? And which revolution?**

The old parties, in particular the Stalinist parties, enter the scene with the intention of putting the brakes on the revolution immediately. In Moscow they formed a so-called freedom committee, mostly composed of captured Nazi generals. The main task of this committee is to suffocate the proletarian revolution like in 1918, form a bourgeois government, and save the capitalist system. If they succeed, then American and English capital and the Russian bureaucracy will dictate a peace to Germany which will make Versailles look like a loving gift. And German capital in turn will dump the entire burden onto the worker.

In this dismal situation the German proletariat does have an ally – **one that it can only win over if it finally stands up for its own interests and fights for them to the end. The establishment of workers' power and the formation of a council government, whose first act will be to expropriate big capital and large estates without compensation, is the only salvation from the growing barbarism of decaying capitalism.** The pioneering struggle[5] of the German working class for socialist revolution will be the catalyst for the proletarian revolution across Europe. The victorious advance of the German revolution will sweep away the counter-revolutionary, chauvinist influence of the Stalin clique everywhere, first of all in Russia itself. It was the defeat of the German working class in 1923 which definitively demoralized the Russian proletariat and placed the bureaucracy in the saddle.

The struggle of the German and European workers for the socialist victory will also help the masses of Russian laborers regain the courage and strength to cast off the bureaucracy in a new revolution, establish soviet democracy, and, following the proletarian states in the advanced countries, free themselves from their miserable situation.

The Union of Socialist Council Republics of Europe, together with the Soviet Union, its hundreds of thousands of agricultural collectives, and its long-planned industries, will become an unassailable bulwark of communism from which it will conquer the world by storm.

The Nazi press, uniformly gagged, reports on a large scale about the mass strikes in England and America. The German workers will not conclude from this – as the propaganda machine, suddenly in love with strikes, wants them to – that the so-called enemy powers have bad prospects, but rather that they themselves have good ones.

That is because they now see that England and America is not just Churchill and Roosevelt, the City and Wall Street, but also the striking workers of Minnesota and Yorkshire. Which of them emerges stronger depends essentially on the attitude of the German worker in the coming revolutionary period.

The formation of the revolutionary party will be indispensable in the struggle to carry out the revolution. The Fourth International was formed before the dissolution of the Third International, in a long, relentless struggle against it. Its communist-internationalist parties fight – openly in the democratic countries, covertly in fascist or occupied territories – for the unification of the revolutionary proletariat. The struggle for the preparation of the new communist-internationalist party in Germany has also begun. *Worker and Soldier* shall be one of the weapons.

May 1, 1944 must be the day of a fateful turning point for the German working class! The rebuilding of the class front must begin! The gun barrels and bayonet points must be turned against the real enemy, our own capital and its agents.

In this sense, illegal proletarian groups of four must be formed in every factory and in every military unit! In these groups, the most active and class-conscious militants must band together. They must follow political developments with the greatest diligence. Wherever proletarians begin to resist the repressive machine, action groups must take the lead of the struggle.

They must also make preparations for the establishment of councils on the day the capitalist war front collapses. On that day, **every factory and every military unit must elect councils** *as the main organs of revolutionary struggle and the basic unit of workers' power!*

For a long time the German workers were at the center of the world proletarian movement. After the defeat of the revolution they lost their central role. Once again, for the coming period, they have returned to the center. **The eyes of the class-conscious proletarians of the world are fixed on them.** *Weakness and half-heartedness will lead the German working class into misery and irrelevance for a long time; confidence in its own strength and courage to fight to the end will make it the champion for the liberation of the world working class and the whole of humanity.*

WORKERS IN OVERALLS AND IN UNIFORM!

On May 1, there will be strikes in the occupied territories and perhaps also workers' demonstrations. The Nazi camarilla will attempt to misuse you as hangman's assistants.

Sabotage these actions!
Refuse to do this henchmen work!
Every shot fired at a European proletarian is a shot fired at the German revolution!
Fraternize with the workers in struggle!
Their cause is your fight!
On May 1, take up the old slogan of common struggle: proletarians of all countries, unite!

GERMAN RAILWAY WORKERS SHOW THE WAY!

A train full of SS men coming from Russia derails. Terrorism or an accident? That hardly mattered to the SS officer. He needed revenge, so he had the French railway workers who came running up put against the wall, and had all the men who could be found in the village snatched and mowed down. What did a few human lives matter to this professional killer who was accustomed to thousands of workers' corpses?

But he had not counted on the fact that the German worker, despite five years of war, has not lost his good sense and solidarity still lives on within him. The German railway workers helped many French people escape, thus saving their lives.

When an investigation later revealed that the accident was not caused by sabotage but rather by the poor condition of the rolling stock, the outrage among the French and German railway workers grew. They resolved to strike for one hour in protest against this murder of innocent workers.

The trains stopped for one hour on this line, with the German railway workers standing by the French workers and in no way obstructing the protest strike.

With their courageous behavior the German railway workers showed that workers do not know national hatred and their solidarity knows no national borders.

When all workers finally understand this and have the courage to act on their convictions, the officers can always give the order: Shoot! the workers, whether in uniform or not, will join hands and march together against the common enemy.

The Fourth International on the march!

Reports of the strikes in Britain have long claimed they broke out against the will of the union bosses and were instigated by dark elements. Finally, Minister Bevin, an honorable member of the Second International, has called this bogeyman by its name. It is the Trotskyists, our comrades from across the Channel.

At the same time the police were ordered to make arrests. Poor Interior Minister! Trying to stop the coming revolution and the growth of the revolutionary party with arrests is like trying to avert a storm tide with a child's rattle.

England's workers are on strike today because they no longer want to endure their misery in the face of the capitalists' billions in profits. The union bosses, of course, are pushing back. The same goes for the English Stalinist party. The Stalin bureaucracy has long since sold out the workers of the world to its allies, English and American capital. Thus only the Trotskyists, the English section of the Fourth International, stand by the English workers in word and deed. They are making the workers aware that their struggle is a preliminary round of the coming revolution, and that it is necessary to prepare for its arrival by closing their ranks.

The *Völkischer Beobachter*[6] makes fun of Mister Bevin. It has no right to. It has still not "observed" that the Trotskyists are playing an active role in workers' struggles in the territories occupied by Gestapo Germany. It believes that police methods and Gestapo terror can forever crush the class struggle in Germany and prevent the emergence of the revolutionary party. Its self-deception will not last much longer.

THE FINANCE MINISTER SPEAKS

The German Finance Minister gave a speech on the radio on April 9 on the topic of war financing. His name is Schwerin-Krosigk and he is a count. This species of animal was not allowed to die by the Republic of Noske and Scheidemann, those butchers of workers. And under the Nazi regime they again fill the most lucrative positions. For example that of the Finance Minister. We give him the floor.

"During the World War, Secretary of State Helfferich[7] had to fight against a divided *Reichstag* [parliament] which shrank from the responsibility for raising urgently needed taxes." Thank you, Mister Minister! At the time, the taxpayer's voice could make itself heard – alas, all too weakly! – in the divided *Reichstag*. Today we have the Gestapo, and that means pay up and don't complain. Now we know what tasks, among others, German big capital has set for the Nazi state. Here is its achievement: "So far we have been able to cover about 50% of the total war costs through taxes." That leaves 50%, which cannot be covered by the money printing press alone. So the usual means must be used, namely credit. This is indeed the case. But how does one get credit? Let's listen.

"Unlike in the First World War, we have not publicly issued war bonds, but rather obtained most of the required credit from banks and other financial institutions" – read savings banks! "Today this is referred to as the method of silent war financing. Its implementation is largely based on the savings made by the German people." So the money the worker takes to the savings bank is forcibly transferred by the savings bank to the state in exchange for a worthless "treasury bond" with no value (a bond on a treasury with no money).[8] The state pays it to the armaments manufacturers so that they can do their honest business with it. But the whole affair has the pretty name silent war financing. The German worker calls it stealing, and he is right. Pickpockets also work silently!

But wait! When the war is over, perhaps everything will be reimbursed, mark for mark and pfennig for pfennig? Indeed: "The German saver who does not now spend his money on superfluous things at inflated prices but takes it to the savings bank is not only doing the right thing regarding the war but also acting wisely." Now he offers the usual promises of the paradise that the Nazis want to establish, if only the final victory is achieved. The count beckons us: have faith in the Nazi state and you shall become its creditor![9] Do not fear inflation, for I already have an effective remedy in the ministerial skull. Let us listen closely to the remedy he discovered there. Here is the gist of the matter.[10]

"The Reich's debts are basically a debt the German people owes to itself. Consequently, at the end of the war the public debt can and will be paid off successfully, partly with tax revenues from the reviving private sector and partly with long-term consolidation." Take note! With your saved money you become your own creditor. This witty Finance Minister is playing a game: My debts, your debts. For the state to pay back its debt to you, you will be bled dry after the war. Since capitalism's first breath, taxes on the private sector have always hit the little guy hardest. So: This gentleman has taken something from you, but in order to give it back he wants to take it again. The remaining debts will be consolidated, which in normal language[11] means: The payment will be put on the back burner.

Alongside Mister Count we have gotten a brief glimpse of the paradise that the Nazi clique and its capitalist backers have planned for us "after the final victory." We are reassured, because this final victory of finance capital will not be achieved. But what did our blue-blooded[12] Finance Minister have in mind? Did he intend, as the *Berliner Börsenzeitung* suggests, to prepare the distinguished public for a new tax increase? Won't they get enough by deducting 30% or more from wages? Or did he simply want to fool working people and incite them to save more?

Then he certainly did a bad job. The workers will not be made April Fools, not even on the ninth! He should have saved his breath so he can cool the hot revolutionary soup that the German proletarians will soon serve up for him, his colleagues, and their capitalist backers.

THE ENEMY IS IN OUR OWN COUNTRY! (Karl Liebknecht)

Notes

1. Karl Liebknecht, "Der Hauptfeind steht im eigenen Land!" *Ausgewählte Reden und Aufsätze* (Berlin: Dietz Verlag, 1952), 296–301; English translation at the Marxists Internet Archive, "The Main Enemy is at Home!" www.marxists.org/archive/liebknecht-k/works/1915/05/main-enemy-home.htm.
2. Literally: "from its high chair," referring to a raised seat for professors.
3. Karl Zörgiebel was a social democratic politician and the Police President of Berlin from 1929–29.
4. A common slogan used not only by Nazis: *Gemeinnutz vor Eigennutz*. The missing part is unintelligible in German: *des grossen Kafelhaftes Geschenk*. It appears the typesetters skipped a line in the manuscript.
5. Literally: *Vorkampf*, a qualifying round in a boxing match.
6. Roughly: National Observer, the central newspaper of the NSDAP from 1920 to 1945.
7. Karl Helrrerich (1872–1924) was secretary of state of the interior in the German Reich from 1916 to 1917.
8. Literally: "a non-existant treasury." This makes more sense in German because the word for treasury is also the word for treasure.
9. A play in words, since "believer" and "creditor" are very similar in German.
10. The German original is a figure of speech from Goethe's Faust I. Faust makes a dog reveal itself as Mephistopheles, and declares: "This is the poodle's kernel!"
11. Literally: "in German."
12. *Krautjunkerlich*, a socialist insult for aristocrats.

PROLETARIANS OF ALL COUNTRIES, UNITE!
SPECIAL ISSUE – JUNE 1944

WORKER and SOLDIER

Organ of the League of Communist-Internationalists (German Section of the fourth International)

THE DECISION IS IN YOUR HANDS!

Soldiers! Comrades![1]

A new and decisive phase of the Second World War has begun. Anglo-American capital has sent its troops to storm the European mainland. With 4000 ships, 13000 planes, and half a million soldiers they have begun the landing on the French Atlantic coast.

"We are prepared for everything." Thus lied the Nazi press, as pompous as ever. They are prepared to take military slaps in the face. Sooner or later the German military machine will have to retreat. American war production alone is vastly superior to German production. The "Allies" could have finished long ago if they had wanted to. But the English and American capitalists – JUST LIKE THE GERMANS – want to prolong the war as long as possible.

The longer the tide of arms deals and billions in profits lasts and the ebb of the post-war sales crisis can be delayed, the better! The more Germany and Russia weaken each other – the finer! The worse the German and Russian proletariat bleed – the nicer!

But the glorious days for the capitalist vultures are coming to an end. The spring offensive has brought the Red Army closer to the German border. The next advance may well bring them into the country, causing the collapse of imperialist Germany. American and English capital would have to move quickly to secure the best position for carving up the spoils.

But the significance of the "second front" does not stop there.

At the same time it is the FRONT OF THE COUNTER-REVOLUTION! The bridgehead between Le Havre and Cherbourg is the bridgehead against the European revolution! The imminent collapse of German imperialism invokes, in an ever more threatening way, the specter of proletarian revolution in Germany and across Europe; a revolution that will leave all previous revolutions in the dust.

Now these gentlemen are showing that they have thought of everything.

A few weeks ago, the British radio station broadcast the real program of these honest fellows. Now they have finally shown their true face. While they were preaching about the happiness and freedom they would bestow on humanity after the war, they were silently preparing the usual means of keeping down the outraged masses in Europe, the bludgeon. To prevent "anarchy," i.e. the emancipation of the working class, and to preserve "order," i.e. the capitalist system of exploitation with crises and wars, they have created an occupation army and a staff of civil inspectors who "all know how to handle machine guns." This plan is to be crowned with the establishment of military governments across Europe.

In Germany they want to replace Hitler with Eisenhower, exchanging one plague for another.

They know what unprecedented misery awaits the workers after the war in a destroyed Germany.

They know that the German worker, squeezed to the limit, will be expected to sweat out double profits, for his own exploiters and for foreign capital.

But they also know that the proletarians of Europe will rise up united against those truly responsible for their poverty: capital and its lackeys.

They imagine that they will be able to deal with this massive revolution with the same old means.

That is why they want to replace the Gestapo executioners with a Scotland Yard expeditionary force.

In this way, our mouths are to be gagged, our hands tied and the whole post-war suffering is to be forced upon on us.

Comrades! Soldiers!

In this situation, the Hitler propaganda calls on us to hold out and defend ourselves. They are really determined to do so themselves.

Hitler in his headquarters, far from the din of the slaughter, Göbbels in his bombproof editorial office, Göring in his Marshall's villa, the entire party camarilla and the rear officers,[2] all are determined to hold out. Stay at the feeding trough as long as possible! Postpone defeat as long as possible, delay the shameful moment when they will be at the mercy of millions of German workers.

They are holding out!

The gentlemen of big capital are also firmly committed. The operations of Krupp, Borsig, and Klöckner, oiled with the blood of German workers, are running quietly at a higher rotational speed and with the greatest efficiency. The capital of the German banks has silently increased from 21 billion in 1939 to 45 billion in 1943. This despite the one hundred percent fraud about a six percent dividend and despite the supposed taxation of war profits. With such earnings, it must be a pleasure to hold out. German capital does not fear being expropriated by its class comrades from across the water. Crows do not peck each other's eyes out. In 1918 everything went well too. At most they will have to share the exploitation of the German worker with their English and American colleagues.

They are holding out!

BUT THE GERMAN SOLDIERS?
THE WORKERS IN UNIFORM?

**They don't want to hold out,
because they can't stand it anymore!**

For almost five years now, they have been sent to the battlefield or to other foreign places, separated from their families, parents, wives, children, and torn away from their workplace. Back home their relatives are being massacred by the murderous arsonists, their hard-earned possessions have been destroyed and their wives have to do heavy labor for a little food and worthless paper money. All that for the billions in profits for the capitalist hyenas and the empty phrases of their Nazi lackeys.

What does the German soldier have to defend?

The Gestapo terror? The socialism of rides on troopships,[3] soup kitchens,[4] overtime, Sunday work, wage deductions, slave driving, the most brazen capitalist exploitation, militarism, great promises, and the Second World War?

Let Hitler and Krupp, Gobbels and Siemens, Goring and Rochling defend their paradise themselves! We want to go back home!

But if we do not want to fight this hopeless battle, does that not mean giving Eisenhower's reactionary force a free ride to Berlin? Hitler or Eisenhower? Are those the only two options?

There is a third: workers' revolution in Germany, Europe, and the world, which would eradicate the capitalist system root and branch, eliminating crises and wars, **and which alone can bring the working masses peace, freedom, and bread.**

Of course, the English and American bourgeoisie intends to bloodily suppress this revolution. To do this it will not be afraid to use the repressive apparatus inherited from German capital, be it police, special troops, or even former Nazi formations.

But there is a gap in the accounting of these gentlemen! **They have not accounted for the English and American workers.**

In the first three months of 1943, the English workers celebrated two hundred thousand strike days. In the same period this year it was almost 2 1/2 million.

Soldiers! Comrades!

Hear these numbers! Understand what they mean! They are a greeting from our fighting class comrades on the other side of the Channel, who are calling over: We, British workers, understand better and better that the capitalists are not fighting this war for the liberation from Stapohitler but rather for their own imperialist interests and profits.

The English workers have also resumed the struggle against misery, war, and capital. **Faced with a proletarian Germany, the**

Churchills and Roosevelts would at most be able to lure the hounds of reaction from the hearth.[5]

But they will need them to deal with their own proletariat.

The question is not: Hitler or Eisenhower, but rather:

Who will defeat Hitler?
EISENHOWER OR THE GERMAN PROLETARIAT?

If the German proletariat topples Hitler before the final military defeat and occupation of Germany and establishes its own organs of power, the workers' and soldiers' councils, everywhere, then the American and British military camarillas will have to openly show before the eyes of the world proletariat who they really are: Not the liberators from the Hitler dictatorship but the stranglers of the European revolution and the sustainers of the military dictatorship of Anglo-American imperialism. The revolutionization of the workers in America and England would thus take a huge step forward.

THE GERMAN REVOLUTION IN RESPONSE TO THE ANGLO-AMERICAN INVASION WILL GIVE THE GERMAN, EUROPEAN, AND WORLD PROLETARIAT A COLOSSAL HEAD START AGAINST WORLD REACTION!

But revolutions do not appear out of thin air.[6] They are prepared by many partial struggles in which the revolutionary class closes its ranks. But today such struggles almost never break out anywhere in Germany. The struggle for the most minimal demands, for food, wages, for the most basic rights and freedoms, protests, strikes, and demonstrations are crushed by the Hitler reaction with the bloodiest terror.

We can only speak one language,
the language of weapons

The German worker holds these in his hands.

But it is of little use for individuals or small units, out of desperation, to take up the struggle alone. They would just make themselves into defenseless victims of the most brutal terror. The struggle must be prepared by organization and assume such a scale that it can become the signal for the revolution in all of Germany. The revolutionary temperature will reach the boiling point after the Anglo-American invasion. In this situation, an uprising by one garrison, in one town or one province, or in one section of the fleet can be the spark that sets off the social explosion.

THE DAY OF THE SAILORS AND DOCKWORKERS OF KIEL WILL RETURN!

But this time around the German revolution will be followed by proletarian uprisings **across Europe**!

Therefore the most important slogan now is:

ORGANIZE YOURSELVES TO PREPARE REVOLUTIONARY STRUGGLES!

Form secret cells of three or four! Admit all workers into these groups who understand the need for proletarian struggle and want to campaign for it!

Soldiers who have the confidence of your units, form committees of revolutionary struggle!

ON EVERY SHIP, IN EVERY BARRACKS, IN EVERY TRENCH, THERE MUST BE REVOLUTIONARY CELLS AND A COMMITTEE OF STRUGGLE!

Connect with fellow soldiers of neighboring units! Encourage them to form cells too!

Get in touch with the local workers, with the French, Belgian and Dutch workers in the West! Our struggle is one!

Remain in constant contact! Only enter the struggle after a mutual understanding! When a struggle breaks out, courageously extend it as much as possible! Spread the news by all means in the country!

Comrades! Soldiers!

If we hope for the days of Kiel to be repeated, then we cannot allow a second Weimar to take place. The workers' and soldiers' councils which on the day of the revolution will cover the rear and the front with a dense network, cannot be dissolved again, but rather must be the foundations of workers' power. In the struggle for the establishment of proletarian power, however, the revolutionary proletarian party is indispensable. The Second and the former Third International, reformists and Stalinists, are planning, on the orders of world capital and the Moscow bureaucracy, to corrode the proletarian revolution from within, as they did in the past. THAT MUST BE THWARTED!

The Fourth International, the Trotskyists in America, England, and the occupied territories of Europe, is standing by the working class in its struggles, despite the terror of the Gestapo and Scotland Yard, and preparing it for tomorrow's revolutionary tasks. In Germany as well, proletarian revolutionaries must gather around this banner and form the nucleus of the new communist-internationalist party.

In the revolutionary cells and committees of struggle, the communists must work together with all workers, even if today they are still reformists or Stalinists, who want to wage the struggle against the existing regime, sincerely and to the end. The further course of the revolution, and the struggle itself, will draw all these comrades to our ranks!

The German workers' response to the invasion of English and American capital must under no circumstances be the defense of Hitler's barbarism! The German workers will respond in "Russian," but not in the manner of Stalin, rather following the example of Lenin and Trotsky.

Their slogan is:

REVOLUTIONARY FRATERNIZATION WITH THE ENGLISH AND AMERICAN SOLDIERS AGAINST GERMAN, AMERICAN AND ENGLISH GENERALS AND THEIR CAPITALIST BACKERS!

REVOLUTIONARY FRATERNIZATION WITH ALL EUROPEAN WORKERS FOR A COMMON STRUGGLE!

PROLETARIAN REVOLUTION IN GERMANY, EUROPE, AND THE WORLD!

Long live the Socialist Council Republic of Germany!

Long live the United Council States of Europe!

Long live the Socialist Council Republic of the World!

Notes

1. German has two words for "comrade": *Genosse* is used by the socialist movement, whereas *Kamerad* is used by the military and the right. This newspaper uses both, and the difference is important. Are the readers being addressed as fellow soldiers or fellow members of the socialist movement? We have translated *Kamerad* as "fellow soldier" to differentiate it from the socialist-tinged *Genosse*.

2. *Etappenoffizier* is an antiquated military term for officers who are responsible behind the front, in contrast to front officers.

3. Literally: "steamboat rides."

4. Literally: "begging soup."

5. This is a German idiom: "To lure the hound from the hearth," i.e. to convince someone to leave a comfortable position.

6. Literally: "are not broken off the fence," referring to grabbing a stick from a medieval fence to win an argument.

PROLETARIANS OF ALL COUNTRIES, UNITE!
JULY 1944

WORKER and SOLDIER

Organ of the League of Communist-Internationalists (German Section of the fourth International)

**DOWN WITH THE WAR
IMMEDIATE PEACE!**

The assassination attempt on Hitler is the last warning call before civil war

The propaganda of the Nazi press sees the hand of providence everywhere. Every day they wait for the miracles without which victory can no longer be expected. Even the assassination attempt that Hitler escaped, carried out by circles of high-ranking officers and a part of big capital, is a sign for the Nazi press that providence is with Hitler. In reality, this assassination attempt shows that circles of high-ranking officers and some of the big bourgeois have realized that Germany is in a hopeless situation and they now want to replace the Hitler state with another bourgeois state. But the Hitler bureaucrats do not want to hand over the reins so quickly; on the contrary, they want to stay at the feeding trough as long as possible. They are defending themselves with the fiercest terror, to practice it freely, Himmler has been given free rein in the big cities of Germany, and even in the occupied territories in the West there have been disturbances and bloody clashes between the Gestapo and the Wehrmacht. The Hitler state is falling apart, so they are calling on the German soldier to hold out to the last.

The fall of Hitler means the German revolution. Only the inhuman terror of the Gestapo, SS, and other gendarmes is forcing the German soldier to remain at the front. All German soldiers and workers have had more than enough of the war; all want to go home. Especially now that they know that victory is unthinkable. For them there is only one slogan:

DOWN WITH THE WAR, IMMEDIATE PEACE!

Hitler can rely on the German army less and less. He has to send Waffen SS, parachute regiments and other shock troops everywhere to stave off collapse.

Signs of discontent in the German army are becoming increasingly visible and numerous. Everywhere one finds fraternization between German soldiers and French and Belgian workers. Many soldiers have defected to the Maquis. The German courts martial have their hands full.

Bloody fighting and retreats on all fronts

The German troops have to yield to the extraordinary pressure of the Americans. But the American and English "saviors" do not want to advance quickly, since such a breakthrough would mean the disintegration of the Normandy front and even the end of the German occupation army, that is to say, the German revolution, which the American capitalists do not want. These monstrous clashes are not only taking place in France; in Italy too the battlefields are getting ever closer to the most important regions. The Red Army is advancing ever further: it is in the heart of the Baltic states, it is marching on Warsaw, and it is on the borders of East Prussia.

Germany is in the most desperate situation

The fraud propaganda, Hitler, Göring, Göbbels place all their hopes of winning the war in God's miracles, providence, and new secret weapons. We have already heard such talk during the war. It was said by the French Prime Minister Paul Reynaud a few weeks before the downfall of France in June 1940. Like Hitler and German capitalism now, he was hoping for a miracle. But it is hopeless. Hitler and his capitalist backers can no longer be saved by a miracle either. Hitler has been pushed back onto his last lines of defense. The domestic situation is getting worse every day. The more hopeless the situation in Germany becomes, the more the capitalists and the bourgeois class are splitting and turning away from Hitler.

But what will come after Hitler?

After five years of pointless mass murder, the soldier at the front and the German worker at home who, under constant threat of being sent to the front, was not allowed to complain, and works under constant bombardment, have had more than enough of the war which has taken from them almost everything they had arduously saved up for. They see that they have nothing to gain in this war. The German soldier, worker, and peasant wants to send the Hitler regime to hell, along with its inhuman Gestapo terror which forces him to shoot at the workers and peasants from the other side. Each man is wondering how he can escape from this hellish war. The Nazi bosses, Göbbels and the like know that the German soldier no longer wants to fight his way through all countries. Therefore, in order to force him to hold out, the propaganda swindlers are warning of the post-war consequences – of a new, even worse Versailles Treaty if Germany loses the war.

All of England's and America's propaganda ultimately comes to Göbbels' aid by incessantly attacking the German soldier, preparing for a military occupation of Germany of indeterminate length with an American military dictatorship (Eisenhower is supposed to rule over the occupied territories of Europe) and even speaking of breaking up the Reich. This is not astonishing. It only proves that the English and American governments are not worth more than the Nazi clique, that they complement each other and that the entirety of capitalist rule, whether in Germany, England, France, or America, must be brought to an end. That can only be accomplished by the victorious revolution of the workers in Germany, Europe, and the world.

The national policy of the former Communist Party helps the reactionary plan of the Americans

But the worst thing is that the plans of the English and American capitalists have found solid backing in the nationalist position of the so-called Communist Party. In Moscou, Staline has created a committee for the "Free Germany" with Hitler generals, barons, and counts who have become prisoners of war. The goal of these gentlemen is to replace the wobbling Hitler regime with a national bourgeois government and thus save German capitalism from the proletarian revolution.

The former Communist Party, the Stalinist degeneration has discarded the Leninist program of international class struggle and international revolution. Staline has dissolved the Comintern, the international leadership of the world revolution, and in all countries has introduced a national policy of attacking the German soldier. The former Communist Party has dropped the policy of revolutionary fraternization in favor of fraternization with our own gang of exploiters; they have united with the reactionary de Gaulle. They make the workers believe that Churchill and Roosevelt will save them. By not calling on the international proletariat to defend the workers' state, instead allying with the largest capitalist states and not calling for the fraternization of the international working class, Staline strengthens Hitler, since German soldiers only encounter hatred everywhere, do not find a solution, and are ultimately pushed back into Hitler's arms, who tells them that Germany must triumph over Europe in order to survive.

Only the transformation of the imperialist war into proletarian revolution can bring peace

Neither Roosevelt-Churchill nor Hitler can bring peace or put an end to the war. Their peace can only be directed against the international working class.

We must put an end to this war: Immediate peace! Only the will of the exploited working masses can put an end to it by taking up the fight against the rule of the capitalists who prepared the war and are responsible for it, who prolong it and who are preparing others for us if we let them do it to us.

Hitler and German capitalism can only be toppled by the working class. The working class must take its destiny in its own hands and turn this imperialist war into a civil war.

All bourgeois parties have already proven their inability to pull Germany out of the crisis; all of them have oppressed the working class and thrown it into ever greater misery. We must not allow the Hitler regime to be replaced with another bourgeois government, however "democratic" it might be, since its main task would be to save German capitalism, which would oppress the workers and peasants even more. Therefore, hang on to your weapons.

The weapons that have been given to you to fight for the interests of the Hitler gang and the German capitalists, you must keep them in a tight grip to turn this imperialist war into a war against capitalism, a civil war. The uprising of the German working class which will establish its workers' and soldiers' councils, and the fraternization with the workers and peasants of Europe, will cast aside all new Versailles Treaties and all the rapacious capitalist plans. The proletarian revolution will thus sweep away capitalism across Europe and in its place establish the United, Socialist Council States of Europe.

Fraternize with the Russian, American, and English soldiers.

Fraternize with the workers of the occupied countries. Do not break the workers' strikes because these represent the struggle against capitalism. On the contrary, show them that you are also workers and peasants, exploited, that you are against the war, against Hitler, and for peace.

Fraternize with the Russian and French prisoners and with the millions of foreign workers who are in Germany and were forced to work far from home, far from their wives and children. Invite them over, communicate with them. In Germany, take up the struggle for better living conditions, against the war, and for peace together.

Form secret cells of three or four! In these cells, discuss the situation in Germany. With slogans spread in secret, fight in your units for better living conditions, for leave, and for all questions that soldiers are asking. Discuss the illegal newspapers and pass them on secretly to other soldiers. Explain the situation in Germany and all of Europe to your fellow soldiers.

Soldiers who have the confidence of your units, form committees of revolutionary struggle. Wherever you can, help the local workers. Seek links with them.

Do not believe that you are isolated. The proletarian revolution is rising in every country in Europe; everywhere the working class is leading a fierce – yet still invisible – struggle against its own exploiters and against the police and fascist terror.

Remain in constant contact! Only enter the struggle after a mutual understanding! When struggle breaks out, courageously extend it as much as possible! Spread the news by all means in the country!

LONG LIVE THE SOCIALIST COUNCIL REPUBLIC OF GERMANY

LONG LIVE THE UNITED COUNCIL STATES OF EUROPE!

LONG LIVE THE SOCIALIST COUNCIL REPUBLIC OF THE WORLD!

IN THE FOOTSTEPS OF KARL LIEBKNECHT AGAINST THE IMPERIALIST WAR

On May 1, 1916, Karl Liebknecht was in Berlin and gave a speech at the Potsdamer Platz. He was arrested and put before a military tribunal. To explain his opinion against the imperialist war he wrote a series of texts; we publish one of the most important here:

The German Government is in its social and historical character an instrument for the crushing down and exploitation of the laboring classes; at home and abroad it serves the interests of junkerism, of capitalism, and of imperialism.

The cry of "Down with the Government!" is meant to brand this entire policy of the Government as fatal to the masses of the people.

This cry also indicates that it is the duty of every representative of the welfare of the proletariat to wage a struggle of the most strenuous character – the class struggle – against the Government.

... The present war is not a war for the defense of the national integrity, not for the liberation of oppressed peoples, not for the welfare of the masses.

From the standpoint of the proletariat this war only signifies the most extreme concentration and extension of political suppression, of economic exploitation, and of military slaughtering of the working-class body and soul for the benefit of capitalism and of absolutism.

To all this the working class of all countries can give but one answer: a harder struggle, the international class struggle against

*the capitalist Governments and the ruling classes of all countries
for the abolition of all oppression and exploitation by the institution
of a peace conceived in the Socialist spirit. In this class struggle the
Socialist, whose Fatherland is the International, finds included the
defense of everything that he, as a Socialist, is bound to defend.*

*The cry of "Down with war" signifies that I thoroughly condemn
and oppose the present war because of its historical nature, because
of its general social causes and specific way in which it originated
(developed), and because of the way it is being carried on and the
objects for which it is being waged. That cry signifies that it is the
duty of every representative of proletarian interests to take part in the
international class struggle for the purpose of ending the war.*[1]

THE CONSCIOUS WORKERS AND THE U.S.S.R.

*The soldier who fought in Russia is confused by the contradictory facts of
Soviet life: on the one hand great, indisputable progress in the cities, new
houses, wide streets, modern and comfortable factories, on the other hand
miserable shacks, mostly in the countryside; peasants living in poverty,
ignorance, and without any comfort. But it is above all the policies of
the leaders of the Soviet Union which confuse the soldiers and German
workers. The chauvinist policies and the collaboration with the worst representatives of world imperialism, Roosevelt and Churchill. How can this
amalgam be explained? The Soviet Union is a workers' state that emerged
from the proletarian revolution of 1917 in which capitalist private property
was expropriated and nationalized.*

*The U.S.S.R., which is a workers' and not a capitalist state, is defending
itself against German imperialism and is fighting a just war in this war.*

The task of every proletarian is to defend it against imperialism.

*But while the U.S.S.R. is a workers' state, it is at the same time a degen-
erated workers' state ruled by a parasite bureaucracy which developed
because of the country's backward character and the delay of the socialist
revolution in other countries.*

*Staline is the representative of this bureaucracy of party and state fonc-
tionaries, of specialists and the military. The conscious workers are for
the U.S.S.R., for the country which thanks to its economic system is closed*

off to imperialist exploitation and which because of the nationalization of private property promotes the development of productive forces.

But conscious workers are at the same time against Stalin's political regime in the U.S.S.R. which is hampering the country's economic progress and is pursuing reactionary policies against the interests of the Soviet people and the international proletariat. The capitalists, fascists, and democrats equate the social regime of the U.S.S.R. with Stalin's current political government. The Stalinists do the same. But the conscious workers who defend the economic order of the U.S.S.R. against the attacks of imperialism in this war, are at the same time fighting against Stalin's political regime. That is, in the U.S.S.R. conscious workers in collaboration for its defense, criticize Stalin's reactionary policies and push the Soviet masses toward the overthrow of the bureaucratic caste that governs.

In the countries allied with the U.S.S.R., they do not allow any calm in the class struggle and proclaim the necessity to overthrow the capitalist regime of Churchill, Roosevelt, and the other "Allies."

In Germany, they are against Hitler and the German capitalist class who supports him and for fraternization with the Red Army and remind them of the task to fight together to overthrow Stalin.

LANDSER [SOLDIER], KEEP YOUR WEAPONS

(Letter from a Soldier)

Fellow soldier, what do you think of the new people who arrived yesterday? Yes – last reserve and again no training, drafted, clothed, pay book, grave tag, and off to the front, but without weapons. As if they had no more weapons at home. But they do.

But listen for a moment. When I was drafted 4 years ago in B, a big industrial town, we too had to wait for our guns and our artillery only arrived after 11 days. How our instructors fumed! Mine, an *Obergefreiter* [senior lance-corporal], a merchant in civilian life and an S.A.man, said: "We have to wait around and over there they always have the newest and best things first." He meant the Waffen SS who had their brand new barracks not far from our camp.

Yes, you know, now he would also understand why the SS always gets everything first, and why the Landser is drafted and immediately shipped to the front without weapons. It is obvious: first of all the Hitler regime is on its last legs, and Hitler and co. are only waiting for a great miracle that will strengthen their rule again, and that's why they have to train their SS at home, because on one hand they can use the SS for advertising among the youth, they're real men, eh?! and then there are the Hitler broads, and the main thing, if the proletariat complains, they can use them alongside the Gestapo for oppression. Yeah, do you really think that they can do that with the new ones at home, then ask them and see what they say?! Rubbish, when that blackguard is gone, Hitler, the war will be over. We are supposed to risk our necks for Hitler and his Nazi bosses, so that they and their backers, German big capital, can continue to rule.

Do you still believe that they can train Landser back home? And with weapons?! The capitalists and their Nazi lackeys are too afraid to do this; they would rather keep the broad masses under their heel with terror, and now where the Red Army is already almost at the border, they are already shitting their pants, so they are shipping the last masses of the worker and peasant proletariat to the front, to the slaughterhouse. They think they can cope with the women and children with their Gestapo executioners. But they can only give weapons to the Landser at the front, where there is no going back for him, where he is forced to shoot forward, and there is no danger that a stray bullet will endanger a Nazi boss, since he only shoots at his peers: the fellow soldier, the comrade from the other side. The officers and reactionary gang stay comfortably under cover. Yes, we're forced to, what are you going to do? Fellow soldier, comrade! I know that you, just like the new ones, all of us, have had it up to here with the frenzied massacre of peoples, with the great slaughter of the international proletariat, but the signal is here, the last hour of the fascist gang has arrived, when Hitler and his criminals will be swept away by the coming social revolution, when these dogs will pay for the crimes they committed against millions of workers. Therefore, fellow soldier, comrade! Protect your weapons! If necessary oil them well again, and don't ever hand them over, since you will need them when the hour strikes, when the capitalists and the fascist gang Hitler, Göring, Himmler, and his Gestapo executioners are swept away by the workers, by you, by us. The gang will no longer leave voluntarily, knowing that all doors are closed to them. They would rather, until their death, destroy the last living thing and the last house along with them! But we will stop this last act of madness by this cowardly brood! Fellow soldiers! When the final hour strikes, we will carry the banner of freedom which will bring us peace and bread, with weapons in our hands, for the socialist revolution, we all want to build the free state of all workers, the free socialist council Germany, from which the socialist revolution will be transferred victoriously to the other countries of Europe, to form a European Union of Councils! Fellow soldier! Comrade! We are standing with arms ready. Until you hear the signal: Let us face the last fight!

FOR A FREE SOCIALIST COUNCIL GERMANY!
FOR A FREE EUROPEAN SOCIALIST UNION OF COUNCILS!
LONG LIVE THE WORLD SOCIALIST REVOLUTION!

Note

1. This is from a letter Liebknecht sent from prison to the military court in response to his charges. It was published in English in 1918 in this collection: Karl Liebknecht, *The Future Belongs to the People: Speeches Made Since the Beginning of the War* (New York: McMillan, 1918), 137–42. The German original was published in Liebknecht's collected works: Karl Liebknecht, *Gesammelte Reden und Schriften*, Band IX (Berlin: Dietz, 1971), 12–16. However, the editors of *Arbeiter und Soldat* used a different German translation. It appears they only had Liebknecht's letter in a different language and translated it back to German. We have taken the original English translation.

[SUMMER 1943]
Work, Freedom, and Bread!
IV. International
Long live the worker!

Newspaper for Soldier and Worker in the West

[...]
[...] answers [...]
[...] I came back from leave a few days ago and I was devastated by the situation in Germany. [What] I saw there [simply] cannot be described. [To begin with,] my hometown has been completely destroyed. There are only a few houses – you can count them – that are still habitable and only a handful that have been spared by the bombs. Then the morality of the population. It's hard to fathom what's going on. Our women and girls have been utterly debauched by the many foreign workers. That is what remains [...] when all the men have been drafted [...] not to mention the food situation. [...] The population must [...] just to get something to survive. [...] Those who don't starve [...] put up with arguments, brawls etc. Then there are the grafters who run a black market almost publicly and offer their dirty goods on the street with a markup of 500–1000 percent. It is catastrophic in Germany. It is probably clear to everyone that the general mood gets worse every day, also that people argue, they almost mutiny, countless brawls occur etc. etc.

In brief, the people want a [...] end of the war.

Fellow soldiers, the way has been shown to me by the IV. International, where you can also help out and contribute to ending the war as quickly as possible. Hear my words, because you, your wives and children are not better off at home. Join us, join the IV. International. We fight for peace – freedom – bread.

A German soldier.

[...]
We've been at war for [...] years now and we can also see [...] the next years too [...]

For 4 years we've been going along everywhere [...] fought, but now I [...] no longer, because I see that the [...] can't stand it anymore. [...] cities [...] in ruins. Thousands of women and children have to sacrifice their precious lives.

Can it go on like this? My wife and also my children write me one letter after the other full of lamentations and I can't help, I can't even console them with an imminent end of the war. My heart turns in my chest when I read and hear this.

I am therefore in favor of putting an end to this abhorrent war. After all, we soldiers can do something for this first and foremost. I know a sure way which is also the right one for you. I cannot do anything on my own, so you have to help and collaborate. Listen and think carefully about the following.

I am in the IV. International and am helping to end the war. We fight against capitalism and for the fraternization of the whole world. With this goal we make it impossible for any state to rule or dictate over Germany in the future, or that it is partitioned among other countries or unnecessary taxes etc. are withheld for one side or another.

Fellow soldiers, because of this IV. International it is ensured that no one, as a result of a revolutionary end of the war, has to fear a different, [...] worse life.

Think of your wives and [children].
Think of a real and [...] peace.
Don't you all want to [participate]?
Join the IV. International!

A fellow soldier

[...]

The starving and tormented proletariat of Europe can only bring a rapid end to its hardship if it breaks completely with world imperialism, rejects any collaboration with its own bourgeoisie and repudiates Stalin's so-called "Holy Union." The liquidation of fascism through the liquidation of capitalism.

Real freedom through the dictatorship of the proletariat.

Only under the flag of the IV. International can the masses [...] this around the world, in Germany, Poland, Spain, Bulgaria, Greece, especially in Italy and France [...] the sections of the IV. International [...] the spread of socialism in Europe, with the proletarian revolution around the world.

IV. International.

Fellow soldiers!

At first it is a bit hard to understand this completely, yet it is nonetheless quite simple. These are only some short slogans of the IV. International. You see the small drawing above which is supposed to show our capitalists in Germany. There are only a few of them, but some of the biggest are included. There are hundreds of these capitalists whose goal is to fill their money bags more and more with our money. The government is under their yoke and must make the necessary propaganda for these capitalist dogs. For the [prolongation] of the war, for more arms, etc. etc. Do we soldiers want to fight for these people? – No. –

Think it over carefully. Join the IV. International
Fight for peace – freedom – work and bread.

Index